AMERICA'S FAVORITES™

Appetizers

Publications International, Ltd.

Pictured on the front cover: Pizza Fondue *(page 14)*.
Pictured on the back cover *(left to right):* Onion, Cheese and Tomato Tart *(page 42)* and Lipton® Roasted Red Pepper & Onion Dip *(page 68)*.

ISBN-13: 978-1-4127-2512-5
ISBN-10: 1-4127-2512-7

Manufactured in China.

8 7 6 5 4 3 2 1

Microwave Cooking: Microwave ovens vary in wattage. Use the cooking times as guidelines and check for doneness before adding more time.

Preparation/Cooking Times: Preparation times are based on the approximate amount of time required to assemble the recipe before cooking, baking, chilling or serving. These times include preparation steps such as measuring, chopping and mixing. The fact that some preparations and cooking can be done simultaneously is taken into account. Preparation of optional ingredients and serving suggestions is not included.

Contents

Maple-Glazed Meatballs

1 ½ cups ketchup

1 cup maple syrup or maple-flavored syrup

⅓ cup reduced-sodium soy sauce

1 tablespoon quick-cooking tapioca

1 ½ teaspoons ground allspice

1 teaspoon dry mustard

2 packages (about 16 ounces each) frozen fully-cooked meatballs

1 can (20 ounces) pineapple chunks in juice, drained

Slow Cooker Directions

1. Combine ketchup, maple syrup, soy sauce, tapioca, allspice and mustard in slow cooker.

2. Partially thaw and separate meatballs. Carefully stir meatballs and pineapple chunks into ketchup mixture.

3. Cover; cook on LOW 5 to 6 hours. Stir before serving. Serve with cocktail picks.

Makes about 48 meatballs

Variation: Serve over hot cooked rice for an entrée.

Prep Time: 10 minutes ✦ *Cook Time:* 5 to 6 hours

Maple-Glazed Meatballs

Spinach Cheese Bundles

1 package (6 ½ ounces) garlic-and-herb spreadable cheese
½ cup chopped fresh spinach
¼ teaspoon black pepper
1 package (17 ¼ ounces) frozen puff pastry, thawed
Sweet-and-sour or favorite dipping sauce (optional)

1. Preheat oven to 400°F. Combine cheese, spinach and pepper in small bowl; mix well.

2. Roll out 1 sheet puff pastry on floured surface into 12-inch square. Cut into 16 (3-inch) squares. Place about 1 teaspoon cheese mixture in center of each square. Brush edges of squares with water. Bring edges together over filling; twist tightly to seal. Fan out corners of puff pastry.

3. Place bundles 2 inches apart on ungreased baking sheets. Bake about 13 minutes or until golden brown. Repeat with remaining sheets of puff pastry and cheese mixture. Serve warm with dipping sauce, if desired.   *Makes 32 bundles*

Cook's Note

If choosing loose spinach, look for leaves with good color and a crisp texture. Avoid limp, wilted, bruised, spotted or discolored leaves. The leaves should have a fresh aroma, not a sour or musty odor. Avoid leaves with thick coarse stems as they are a sign of overgrown spinach, which can be tough and bitter.

7

Spinach Cheese Bundles

Apricot BBQ Glazed Shrimp and Bacon

  1 can (8 ounces) sliced water chestnuts, drained
36 raw medium shrimp, peeled and deveined (about 1 ¼ pounds)
  9 bacon slices, each cut into 4 pieces
⅓ cup barbecue sauce
⅓ cup apricot fruit spread
  1 tablespoon grated fresh ginger
  1 tablespoon cider vinegar
⅛ teaspoon red pepper flakes

1. Preheat broiler. Place 1 water chestnut slice on top of each shrimp. Wrap 1 piece of bacon around shrimp and secure with wooden toothpick. Repeat with remaining water chestnuts, shrimp and bacon.

2. Line broiler pan with foil; insert broiler rack. Coat broiler rack with nonstick cooking spray. Place shrimp on rack.

3. Combine remaining ingredients in small bowl. Brush sauce evenly over shrimp. Broil 2 minutes; turn. Baste and broil 2 minutes more; turn again. Baste and broil 1 minute more or until edges of bacon begin to brown.   *Makes 36 appetizers*

Apricot BBQ Glazed Shrimp and Bacon

Bacon-Wrapped Breadsticks

   8 slices bacon

16 garlic-flavored breadsticks (about 8 inches long)

³/₄ cup grated Parmesan cheese

   2 tablespoons chopped fresh parsley (optional)

1. Cut bacon slices in half lengthwise. Wrap half slice of bacon diagonally around each breadstick. Combine Parmesan cheese and parsley, if desired, in shallow dish; set aside.

2. Place 4 breadsticks on double layer of paper towels in microwave oven. Microwave at HIGH 2 to 3 minutes or until bacon is cooked through. Immediately roll breadsticks in Parmesan mixture to coat. Repeat with remaining breadsticks.

Makes 16 breadsticks

Sweet and Spicy Sausage Rounds

   1 pound Kielbasa sausage, cut into ¹/₄-inch rounds

²/₃ cup blackberry jam

¹/₃ cup steak sauce

   1 tablespoon prepared mustard

¹/₂ teaspoon ground allspice

Slow Cooker Directions

1. Place all ingredients in slow cooker; toss to coat completely. Cook on HIGH 3 hours or until richly glazed.

2. Serve with cocktail picks for appetizers or over rice tossed with chopped green onion for an entrée.

Makes 3 cups

Bacon-Wrapped Breadsticks

Country French Eggs

6 hard-cooked eggs, peeled and sliced in half lengthwise

2 tablespoons milk

1 tablespoon minced fresh tarragon *or* 1 teaspoon dried tarragon leaves

1 clove garlic, minced

1/8 teaspoon salt

1/8 teaspoon black pepper

2 teaspoons Dijon mustard

2 teaspoons tarragon vinegar

1 teaspoon honey

Dash salt

Dash black pepper

1 tablespoon olive oil

1 tablespoon butter

Fresh tarragon sprigs (optional)

1. Remove yolks from egg halves. Mash yolks in small bowl. Add milk, minced tarragon, garlic, 1/8 teaspoon salt and 1/8 teaspoon pepper; mix well. Reserve 2 tablespoons yolk mixture. Fill egg halves with remaining yolk mixture, patting firmly into each egg.

2. Add mustard, vinegar, honey, dash salt and dash pepper to reserved yolk mixture. Whisk in oil, pouring in thin stream; set aside.

3. Heat butter in large skillet over medium-low heat. Place egg halves, yolk-side down, in skillet. Cook 2 to 3 minutes or until yolk mixture is slightly golden. *Do not overcook egg yolks or whites.*

4. Pour yolk-mustard mixture onto serving plate. Place cooked egg halves on plate over dressing. Garnish with tarragon sprigs, if desired.

Makes 6 servings (2 halves per serving)

Add a Special Touch: For a more elegant breakfast or brunch entrée, add bits of cooked fish, shellfish, spinach, or chopped mushrooms to the mashed yolk mixture before filling the egg halves.

Honey Nut Brie

¼ cup honey

¼ cup coarsely chopped pecans

1 tablespoon brandy (optional)

1 wheel (14 ounces) Brie cheese (about 5-inch diameter)

1. Combine honey, pecans and brandy, if desired, in small bowl. Place cheese on large round ovenproof platter or in 9-inch pie plate.

2. Bake in preheated 500°F oven 4 to 5 minutes or until cheese softens. Drizzle honey mixture over top of cheese. Bake 2 to 3 minutes longer or until topping is thoroughly heated. *Do not melt cheese.*   *Makes 16 to 20 servings*

Tip: Serve this party dish with crackers, tart apple wedges and seedless grapes.

Mediterranean Roast Tomatoes

2 small to medium beefsteak tomatoes, cut in half crosswise

4 fresh basil leaves

2 tablespoons finely chopped pitted kalamata olives

2 tablespoons shredded reduced-fat mozzarella cheese

2 tablespoons grated Parmesan cheese

1. Preheat toaster oven to broil. Place tomato halves on toaster oven tray or on toaster-sized broiler pan. Top each tomato half with 1 fresh basil leaf, 1 ½ teaspoons olives, 1 ½ teaspoons mozzarella cheese and 1 ½ teaspoons Parmesan cheese.

2. Broil in toaster oven 2 minutes or until cheese melts and begins to brown. Let cool slightly before serving.   *Makes 4 servings*

Pizza Fondue

½ pound bulk Italian sausage

1 cup chopped onion

2 jars (26 ounces each) meatless pasta sauce

4 ounces thinly sliced ham, finely chopped

1 package (3 ounces) sliced pepperoni, finely chopped

¼ teaspoon red pepper flakes

1 pound mozzarella cheese, cut into ¾-inch cubes

1 loaf Italian or French bread, cut into 1-inch cubes

Slow Cooker Directions

1. Cook sausage and onion in large skillet until sausage is browned. Drain off fat.

2. Transfer sausage mixture to slow cooker. Stir in pasta sauce, ham, pepperoni and red pepper flakes. Cover; cook on LOW 3 to 4 hours.

3. Serve fondue with cheese cubes, bread cubes and fondue forks.

Makes 20 to 25 appetizer servings

Prep Time: 15 minutes ✦ Cook Time: 3 to 4 hours

Cook's Note

Serve Pizza Fondue with chunks of red and green pepper, mushrooms or your favorite vegetable pizza topping.

Pizza Fondue

15

Tiny Spinach Quiches

Pastry

    1 package (3 ounces) cream cheese, softened

    $1/2$ cup butter or margarine, softened

    1 cup all-purpose flour

Filling

    5 slices bacon, cooked and crumbled

    1 cup grated Swiss cheese

    1 can (13.5 ounces) POPEYE® Chopped Spinach, drained

    3 eggs

    $3/4$ cup light cream

    $1/4$ teaspoon nutmeg

       Salt and pepper to taste

1. To prepare pastry: Cut cream cheese and butter into flour. Form into a ball; wrap in plastic wrap and chill 1 hour. Lightly flour rolling pin. Place pastry on lightly floured work surface, roll out to $1/8$-inch thickness and cut into 16 circles with 3-inch biscuit cutter. Line sixteen $1 1/2$-inch plain or fluted muffin pan cups, or mini-muffin pan cups, with dough circles.

2. To prepare filling: Preheat oven to 375°F. Sprinkle bacon, then cheese, evenly over bottoms of unbaked pastries. Squeeze spinach dry and spread evenly over bacon and cheese. In medium bowl, combine remaining ingredients. Pour evenly into pastry cups. Bake 30 minutes or until set.   *Makes 16 appetizers*

Note: To serve as a pie, pour filling into one 9-inch frozen ready-to-bake pie crust.

Tiny Spinach Quiches

Toasted Pesto Rounds

1/4 cup thinly sliced fresh basil or chopped fresh dill

1/4 cup grated Parmesan cheese

3 tablespoons reduced-fat mayonnaise

1 medium clove garlic, minced

12 French bread slices, about 1/4 inch thick

1 tablespoon plus 1 teaspoon chopped fresh tomato

1 green onion with top, sliced

Black pepper

1. Preheat broiler.

2. Combine basil, cheese, mayonnaise and garlic in small bowl; mix well.

3. Arrange bread slices in single layer on large ungreased nonstick baking sheet or broiler pan. Broil 6 to 8 inches from heat 30 to 45 seconds or until bread slices are lightly toasted.

4. Turn bread slices over; spread evenly with basil mixture. Broil 1 minute or until lightly browned. Top evenly with tomato and green onion. Season to taste with pepper. Transfer to serving plate.

Makes 12 servings

Toasted Pesto Rounds

Antipasto Crescent Bites

2 ounces cream cheese (do not use reduced-fat or fat-free cream cheese)
1 package (8 ounces) refrigerated crescent roll dough
1 egg plus 1 tablespoon water, beaten
4 (3 × ¾-inch) strips roasted red pepper
2 large marinated artichoke hearts, cut in half lengthwise to ¾-inch width
1 thin slice Genoa or other salami, cut into 4 strips
4 small stuffed green olives, cut into halves

1. Preheat oven to 375°F. Cut cream cheese into 16 equal pieces, about 1 teaspoon per piece; set aside.

2. Remove dough from package. Unroll on lightly floured surface. Cut each dough triangle in half lengthwise to form 2 triangles. Brush edges of triangles lightly with egg mixture.

3. Wrap 1 red pepper strip around 1 piece of cream cheese. Place on dough triangle; fold over and pinch edges to seal. Place 1 piece of artichoke heart and 1 piece of cream cheese on dough triangle; fold over and pinch edges to seal. Wrap 1 salami strip around 1 piece of cream cheese. Place on dough triangle; fold over and pinch edges to seal. Place 2 olive halves and 1 piece of cream cheese on dough triangle; fold over and pinch edges to seal. Repeat with remaining red pepper strips, artichoke pieces, salami strips, olives, cream cheese and dough triangles. Place filled triangles evenly spaced on ungreased baking sheet. Brush with egg mixture.

4. Bake 12 to 14 minutes or until golden brown. Cool on wire rack. Store in airtight container in refrigerator.

5. Reheat on baking sheet in preheated 325°F oven 7 to 8 minutes or until warmed through. Do not microwave.   *Makes 16 pieces*

Antipasto Crescent Bites

Beefy Stuffed Mushrooms

1 pound 90% lean ground beef

2 teaspoons prepared horseradish

1 teaspoon chopped fresh chives

1 clove garlic, minced

1/4 teaspoon black pepper

18 large mushrooms

2/3 cup dry white wine

1. Preheat oven to 350°F. Thoroughly mix ground beef, horseradish, chives, garlic and pepper in medium bowl.

2. Remove stems from mushrooms; stuff mushroom caps with beef mixture.

3. Place stuffed mushrooms in shallow baking dish; pour wine over mushrooms. Bake 20 minutes or until meat is browned. *Makes 1 1/2 dozen mushrooms*

Pimiento Cheese Toast

1 loaf French bread

1 cup (4 ounces) shredded reduced-fat sharp Cheddar cheese

2 tablespoons diced pimiento

2 tablespoons reduced-fat mayonnaise

1 teaspoon lemon juice

1/4 teaspoon dried oregano

1. Slice bread into 8 (1-inch-thick) slices. Toast lightly in toaster or toaster oven.

2. Combine cheese and pimiento in medium bowl. Combine mayonnaise, lemon juice and oregano in small bowl; stir into cheese mixture. Spread 1 tablespoon mixture onto each slice of toast.

3. Preheat broiler. Place prepared toasts on broiler rack. Broil, 4 inches from heat, 2 minutes. Serve immediately. *Makes 8 servings*

Venetian Canapés

12 slices firm white bread

5 tablespoons butter or margarine, divided

2 tablespoons all-purpose flour

$^1/_2$ cup milk

3 ounces fresh mushrooms (about 9 medium), finely chopped

6 tablespoons grated Parmesan cheese, divided

2 teaspoons anchovy paste

$^1/_4$ teaspoon salt

$^1/_8$ teaspoon black pepper

Green and ripe olive slices, red and green bell pepper strips and rolled anchovy fillets, for garnish (optional)

1. Preheat oven to 350°F. Cut 2 rounds out of each bread slice with 2-inch round cutter. Melt 3 tablespoons butter in small saucepan. Brush both sides of bread rounds lightly with butter. Bake bread rounds on ungreased baking sheet 5 to 6 minutes per side or until golden. Remove to wire rack. Cool completely. *Increase oven temperature to 425°F.*

2. Melt remaining 2 tablespoons butter in same small saucepan. Stir in flour; cook and stir over medium heat until bubbly. Whisk in milk; cook and stir 1 minute or until sauce thickens and bubbles. (Sauce will be very thick.) Place mushrooms in large bowl; stir in sauce, 3 tablespoons cheese, anchovy paste, salt and black pepper until well blended.

3. Spread 1 heaping teaspoonful mushroom mixture onto each toast round; place on ungreased baking sheets. Sprinkle remaining 3 tablespoons cheese over bread rounds, dividing evenly. Bake 5 to 7 minutes or until tops are light brown. Serve warm. Garnish, if desired.   *Makes 8 to 10 appetizer servings*

Easy Spinach Appetizer

2 tablespoons butter

3 eggs

1 cup milk

1 cup all-purpose flour

1 teaspoon baking powder

1 teaspoon salt

2 packages (10 ounces each) frozen chopped spinach, thawed and well drained

4 cups (16 ounces) shredded Monterey Jack cheese

1/2 cup diced red bell pepper

1. Preheat oven to 350°F. Melt butter in 13×9-inch pan.

2. Beat eggs in medium bowl. Add milk, flour, baking powder and salt; beat until well blended. Stir in spinach, cheese and bell pepper; mix well. Spread mixture over melted butter in pan.

3. Bake 40 to 45 minutes or until set. Let stand 10 minutes before cutting into triangles or squares. *Makes 2 to 4 dozen pieces*

Tip: Easy Spinach Appetizer can also be made ahead, frozen and reheated. After baking, cool completely and cut into squares. Transfer squares to cookie sheet; place cookie sheet in freezer until squares are frozen solid. Transfer to resealable plastic food storage bag. To serve, reheat squares in preheated 325°F oven for 15 minutes.

Easy Spinach Appetizer

Turkey Meatballs in Cranberry-Barbecue Sauce

1 can (16 ounces) jellied cranberry sauce

1/2 cup barbecue sauce

1 egg white

1 pound 93% lean ground turkey

1 green onion with top, sliced

2 teaspoons grated orange peel

1 teaspoon reduced-sodium soy sauce

1/4 teaspoon black pepper

1/8 teaspoon ground red pepper (optional)

Nonstick cooking spray

Slow Cooker Directions

1. Combine cranberry sauce and barbecue sauce in slow cooker. Cover; cook on HIGH 20 to 30 minutes or until cranberry sauce is melted and mixture is hot.

2. Meanwhile, place egg white in medium bowl; beat lightly. Add turkey, green onion, orange peel, soy sauce, black pepper and ground red pepper, if desired; mix until well blended. Shape into 24 balls.

3. Spray large nonstick skillet with cooking spray. Add meatballs to skillet; cook over medium heat 8 to 10 minutes or until meatballs are no longer pink in center, carefully turning occasionally to brown evenly. Add to heated sauce in slow cooker; stir gently to coat.

4. Reduce heat to LOW. Cover; cook 3 hours. Transfer meatballs to serving plate; garnish, if desired. Serve with decorative picks. *Makes 12 servings*

Turkey Meatballs in Cranberry-Barbecue Sauce

Spicy Sweet & Sour Cocktail Franks

2 packages (8 ounces each) cocktail franks

½ cup ketchup or chili sauce

½ cup apricot preserves

1 teaspoon hot pepper sauce

Additional hot pepper sauce (optional)

Slow Cooker Directions

1. Combine all ingredients in slow cooker; mix well. Cover; cook on LOW 2 to 3 hours.

2. Serve warm or at room temperature with cocktail picks and additional hot pepper sauce, if desired.   *Makes about 4 dozen cocktail franks*

Prep Time: 8 minutes ◆ Cook Time: 2 to 3 hours

28

Cook's Note

Keep the lid on! The slow cooker can take as long as 30 minutes to regain heat lost when the cover is removed. Only remove the cover when instructed to do so by the recipe.

Spicy Sweet & Sour Cocktail Franks

Individual Spinach & Bacon Quiches

  3 slices bacon
¹/₂ small onion, diced
  1 package (9 ounces) frozen chopped spinach, thawed, drained and squeezed dry
¹/₂ teaspoon black pepper
¹/₈ teaspoon ground nutmeg
  Pinch salt
  1 container (15 ounces) whole milk ricotta cheese
  2 cups (8 ounces) shredded mozzarella cheese
  1 cup grated Parmesan cheese
  3 eggs, lightly beaten

1. Preheat oven to 350°F. Spray 10 muffin pan cups with nonstick cooking spray.

2. Cook bacon in large skillet over medium-high heat until crisp. Drain on paper towels. Let bacon cool; crumble.

3. In same skillet, cook and stir onion in remaining bacon fat 5 minutes or until tender. Add spinach, pepper, nutmeg and salt. Cook and stir over medium heat about 3 minutes or until liquid evaporates. Remove from heat. Stir in bacon; cool.

4. Combine ricotta, mozzarella and Parmesan cheeses in large bowl. Add eggs; stir until well blended. Add cooled spinach mixture; mix well.

5. Divide mixture evenly among prepared muffin cups. Bake 40 minutes or until filling is set. Let stand 10 minutes. Run thin knife around edges to release. Serve hot or refrigerate and serve cold.

Makes 10 servings

Individual Spinach & Bacon Quiches

Tomato and Caper Crostini

1 French roll, cut into 8 slices (about 1 1/2 ounces)
2 plum tomatoes, finely chopped (about 4 ounces)
1 1/2 tablespoons capers
1 1/2 teaspoons dried basil leaves
1 teaspoon extra-virgin olive oil
1 ounce crumbled feta (any variety, preferably sun-dried tomatoes and basil)

1. Preheat oven to 350°F.

2. Place bread slices on ungreased baking sheet in single layer. Bake 15 minutes or just until golden brown. Cool completely.

3. Meanwhile, combine tomatoes, capers, basil and oil in small bowl.

4. At serving time, spoon tomato mixture onto each bread slice; sprinkle with cheese.

Makes 2 servings

Cook's Note

Bread slices can be made ahead of time. Cool completely and store in a plastic resealable food storage bag.

Tomato and Caper Crostini

Arugula-Prosciutto Wrapped Breadsticks with Garlic Mustard Sauce

1/2 cup mayonnaise

6 tablespoons grated Parmesan cheese

2 tablespoons *French's*® Honey Dijon Mustard

1 tablespoon chopped fresh basil

2 teaspoons minced garlic

1 package (4 1/2 ounces) long breadsticks (12 to 16 breadsticks)

1 1/3 cups *French's*® French Fried Onions, crushed

1/2 pound thinly sliced prosciutto or smoked deli ham

1 bunch arugula (about 20 leaves) or green leaf lettuce, washed, drained and stems removed

1. Combine mayonnaise, cheese, mustard, basil and garlic in mixing bowl. Spread half of each breadstick with some of mustard sauce. Roll in French Fried Onions, pressing firmly.

2. Arrange prosciutto slices on flat work surface. Top each slice with leaf of arugula. Place coated end of breadsticks on top; roll up jelly-roll style. Place seam side down on serving platter.

3. Serve wrapped breadsticks with remaining mustard sauce for dipping.

Makes 16 appetizers

Prep Time: 25 minutes

Sweet Glazed Meatballs

1 pound lean ground beef
1/2 cup quick-cooking oats
1/2 cup finely minced yellow onion
2 large eggs, beaten
1 teaspoon salt
1/2 teaspoon Worcestershire sauce
1/4 teaspoon black pepper
3 tablespoons CRISCO® Oil
1/2 cup SMUCKER'S® Low Sugar Concord Grape Reduced Sugar Jelly
1/2 cup chili sauce
1/4 teaspoon ground allspice

1. Combine ground beef, oats, onion, eggs, salt, Worcestershire and pepper in a large bowl; mix well. Shape into 36 (1 1/4-inch) meatballs.

2. Heat CRISCO® Oil in a 12-inch skillet over medium heat until hot. Add meatballs and cook 10 minutes or until browned, turning frequently. (Use two utensils for easier handling.) Drain on paper towels and discard any pan drippings.

3. In a small bowl, combine remaining ingredients and whisk until smooth.

4. Wipe skillet clean with paper towels. Return meatballs to skillet, pour SMUCKER'S® Jelly mixture over the meatballs and cook, uncovered, over medium heat 15 minutes or until richly glazed, stirring occasionally. Serve with wooden picks.

Makes 3 dozen meatballs

Leek Strudels

Butter-flavored nonstick cooking spray

2 pounds leeks, cleaned and sliced (white parts only)

1/4 teaspoon salt

1/4 teaspoon caraway seeds

1/8 teaspoon white pepper

1/4 cup fat-free reduced-sodium chicken broth

3 sheets frozen phyllo dough, thawed

1. Coat large skillet with cooking spray; heat over medium heat. Add leeks; cook and stir about 5 minutes or until tender. Stir in salt, caraway seeds and pepper. Add chicken broth; bring to a boil over high heat. Reduce heat to low. Simmer, covered, about 5 minutes or until broth is absorbed. Let cool to room temperature.

2. Preheat oven to 400°F. Cut each sheet of phyllo dough lengthwise into thirds. Spray 1 piece phyllo dough with cooking spray; spoon 2 tablespoons leek mixture near bottom of piece. Fold 1 corner over filling to make triangle. Continue folding, as you would fold a flag, to make triangular packet.

3. Repeat with remaining phyllo dough and leek mixture. Place packets on ungreased baking sheet; lightly coat tops of packets with cooking spray. Bake about 20 minutes or until golden brown. Serve warm.   *Makes 9 servings*

Leek Strudels

Sweet and Sour Hot Dog Bites

¹/₂ cup **SMUCKER'S®** Grape Jelly

¹/₄ cup **prepared mustard**

1 **tablespoon sweet pickle relish**

¹/₂ pound **frankfurters, cooked**

In a saucepan, combine SMUCKER'S® Jelly, mustard, and relish.

Heat over very low heat, stirring constantly, until mixture is hot and well blended.

Slice frankfurters diagonally into bite-size pieces. Add to sauce and heat thoroughly.

Makes 20 snack servings

38

Cook's Note

At your party, use a small-sized (1-quart) slow cooker on a low setting to keep these hot dog bites warm.

Sweet and Sour Hot Dog Bites

Rosemary-Roasted Vegetable Crostini

1 small eggplant (about ³/₄ pound)

1 medium zucchini

1 medium red onion

1 medium green bell pepper

2 Italian plum tomatoes, seeded

¹/₄ cup dry white wine or orange juice

2 tablespoons tarragon white wine vinegar

4 medium cloves garlic, minced

1 tablespoon olive oil

1 tablespoon chopped fresh rosemary *or* 1 teaspoon dried rosemary, crushed

¹/₄ teaspoon black pepper

1 loaf (1 pound) sourdough bread, 12 to 14 inches long

1 cup (4 ounces) shredded part-skim mozzarella cheese

40

1. Preheat oven to 400°F. Spray large nonstick baking sheets with nonstick cooking spray; set aside.

2. Trim ends from eggplant and zucchini; discard. Cut all vegetables into ¹/₄-inch pieces. Place vegetables in large bowl. Add wine, vinegar, garlic, oil and seasonings; toss to coat evenly. Transfer to ungreased nonstick 15×10×1-inch jelly-roll pan.

3. Bake 45 minutes or until lightly browned, stirring every 15 minutes.

4. Trim and discard ends from bread. Cut bread into ¹/₂-inch-thick slices. Arrange slices in single layer on prepared baking sheets. Bake 3 minutes on each side or until crisp and lightly browned on both sides.

5. Spoon vegetable mixture evenly onto toasted bread slices; sprinkle evenly with cheese. Continue baking 5 minutes or until mixture is heated through and cheese is melted. Transfer to serving plates; garnish, if desired. *Makes 12 servings*

Rosemary-Roasted Vegetable Crostini

Onion, Cheese and Tomato Tart

Parmesan-Pepper Dough (recipe follows)
1 **tablespoon butter**
1 **medium onion, thinly sliced**
1 **cup (4 ounces) shredded Swiss cheese**
2 **to 3 ripe tomatoes, sliced**
   Black pepper
2 **tablespoons chopped fresh chives**

1. Prepare Parmesan-Pepper Dough.

2. Melt butter in large skillet over medium heat. Add onion; cook and stir 20 minutes or until tender.

3. Spread onion over prepared dough. Sprinkle with cheese. Let rise in warm place 20 to 30 minutes or until edges are puffy.

4. Preheat oven to 400°F. Top dough with tomatoes. Sprinkle with pepper. Bake 25 minutes or until edges are deep golden and cheese is melted. Let cool 10 minutes. Transfer to serving platter. Sprinkle with chives. Cut into wedges.

Makes 6 to 8 servings

Parmesan-Pepper Dough

1 package ($\frac{1}{4}$ ounce) active dry yeast

1 tablespoon sugar

$\frac{2}{3}$ cup warm water (105° to 115°F)

2 cups all-purpose flour, divided

$\frac{1}{4}$ cup grated Parmesan cheese

1 teaspoon salt

$\frac{1}{2}$ teaspoon black pepper

1 tablespoon olive oil

1. Sprinkle yeast and sugar over warm water in small bowl; stir until yeast is dissolved. Let stand 5 minutes or until mixture is bubbly.

2. Combine 1$\frac{3}{4}$ cups flour, cheese, salt and pepper in large bowl. Pour yeast mixture and oil over flour mixture and stir until mixture clings together.

3. Turn out dough onto lightly floured surface. Knead 8 to 10 minutes or until smooth and elastic, adding remaining $\frac{1}{4}$ cup flour if necessary. Shape dough into ball; place in large greased bowl. Turn dough so that top is greased. Cover with towel; let rise in warm place 1 hour or until doubled in bulk.

4. Punch down dough. Knead on lightly floured surface 1 minute or until smooth. Flatten into disc. Roll dough to make 11-inch round. Press into bottom and up side of buttered 9- or 10-inch tart pan with removable bottom.

43

Skewered Antipasto

1 jar (8 ounces) SONOMA® marinated dried tomatoes

1 pound (3 medium) new potatoes, cooked until tender

2 cups bite-sized vegetable pieces (such as celery, bell peppers, radishes, carrots, cucumber and green onions)

1 cup drained cooked egg tortellini and/or spinach tortellini

1 tablespoon chopped fresh chives *or* 1 teaspoon dried chives

1 tablespoon chopped fresh rosemary *or* 1 teaspoon dried rosemary

Drain oil from tomatoes into medium bowl. Place tomatoes in small bowl; set aside. Cut potatoes into 1-inch cubes. Add potatoes, vegetables, tortellini, chives and rosemary to oil in medium bowl. Stir to coat with oil; cover and marinate 1 hour at room temperature. To assemble, alternately thread tomatoes, potatoes, vegetables and tortellini onto 6-inch skewers.   *Makes 12 to 14 skewers*

Cook's Note

New potatoes may be any variety, but most often are round reds.

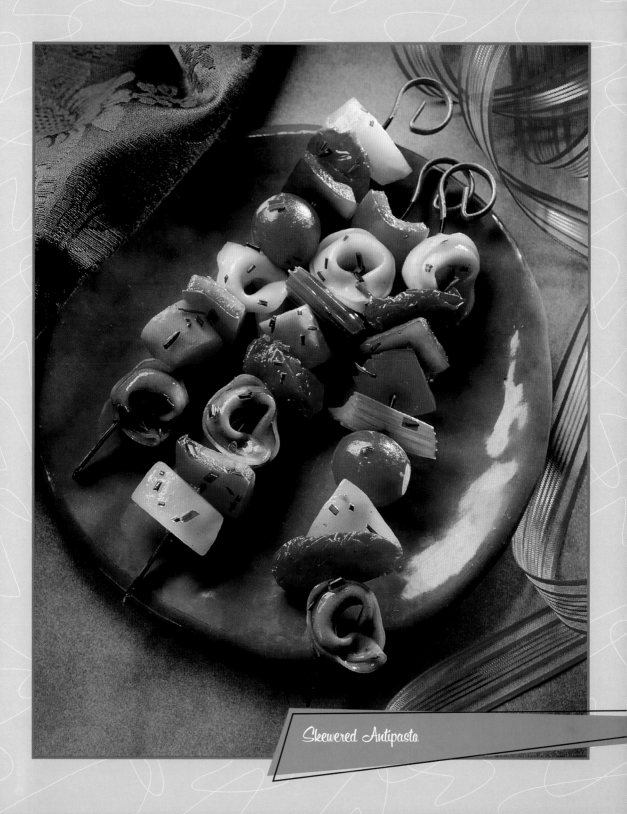

Skewered Antipasto

Pinwheel Ham Bites

2 packages (6 ½ ounces) garlic-and-herb spreadable cheese, softened
4 (¹⁄₁₆-inch-thick) slices boiled ham
40 round buttery crackers

1. Spread ½ package cheese to edges of each ham slice. Beginning at short end, roll up tightly. Wrap tightly in plastic wrap; refrigerate rolls at least 2 hours.

2. Cut each roll crosswise into 10 slices. Place 1 slice on each cracker. Serve immediately. *Makes 40 appetizers*

Prep Time: 30 minutes ✦ Chill Time: 2 hours

Pinwheel Ham Bites

Confetti Tuna in Celery Sticks

1 (3-ounce) pouch of STARKIST Flavor Fresh Pouch® Albacore or Chunk Light Tuna

1/2 cup shredded red or green cabbage

1/2 cup shredded carrots

1/4 cup shredded yellow squash or zucchini

3 tablespoons reduced-calorie cream cheese, softened

1 tablespoon plain low-fat yogurt

1/2 teaspoon dried basil, crushed

Salt and pepper to taste

10 to 12 (4-inch) celery sticks, with leaves if desired

In a small bowl toss together tuna, cabbage, carrots and squash.

Stir in cream cheese, yogurt and basil. Add salt and pepper to taste.

With small spatula spread mixture evenly into celery sticks.

Makes 10 to 12 servings

48

Prep Time: 20 minutes

Confetti Tuna in Celery Sticks

Dilly Deviled Eggs

6 hard-cooked eggs, peeled and sliced in half lengthwise

1 tablespoon reduced-fat sour cream

1 tablespoon low-fat mayonnaise

1 tablespoon low-fat (1%) cottage cheese

1 tablespoon minced fresh dill *or* **1** teaspoon dried dill weed

1 tablespoon minced dill pickle

1 teaspoon Dijon mustard

¹/₈ teaspoon salt

¹/₈ teaspoon white pepper

Paprika for garnish

Dill sprigs for garnish (optional)

1. Remove yolks from egg halves. Mash yolks with sour cream, mayonnaise, cottage cheese, dill, pickle, Dijon mustard, salt and pepper in small bowl.

2. Fill egg halves with mixture, using teaspoon or piping bag fitted with large, plain tip. Garnish filled egg halves with paprika and dill sprigs, if desired.

Makes 6 servings

50

Marinated Mushrooms

2 pounds mushrooms
1 bottle (**8 ounces**) Italian salad dressing
  Grated peel of ¹/₂ **SUNKIST**® lemon
  Juice of **1 SUNKIST**® lemon
2 tablespoons sliced pimiento (**optional**)
2 tablespoons chopped fresh parsley

In large saucepan, combine mushrooms and Italian dressing; bring to a boil. Cook, uncovered, 2 to 3 minutes, stirring constantly. Add lemon peel, juice and pimiento. Chill 4 hours or more. Drain, reserving dressing for another use. Stir parsley into mushrooms. Serve as an appetizer with toothpicks. Garnish with lemon cartwheel slices, if desired. *Makes about 4 cups*

Note: Reserved dressing may be used on salads. Makes about 1 ¹/₂ cups.

Cook's Note

Substitute 1 bottle (8 ounces) reduced-calorie Italian dressing for regular Italian dressing.

Smoked Salmon Roses

1 package (8 ounces) cream cheese, softened
1 tablespoon prepared horseradish
1 tablespoon minced fresh dill plus whole sprigs for garnish
1 tablespoon half-and-half
16 slices (12 to 16 ounces) smoked salmon
1 red bell pepper, cut into thin strips

1. Combine cream cheese, horseradish, minced dill and half-and-half in small bowl. Beat until light and creamy.

2. Spread 1 tablespoon cream cheese mixture over each salmon slice. Roll up jelly-roll style. Slice each roll in half crosswise. Arrange salmon rolls, cut sides down, on serving dish to resemble roses. Garnish each "rose" by tucking 1 pepper strip and 1 dill sprig in center.

Makes 32 "roses"

52

Zesty Liver Pâté

$1/3$ cup butter or margarine
1 pound chicken livers
$3/4$ cup coarsely chopped green onions
$3/4$ cup chopped fresh parsley
$1/2$ cup dry white wine
$3/4$ teaspoon TABASCO® brand Pepper Sauce
$1/2$ teaspoon salt
   Crackers or French bread

Melt butter in large saucepan; add chicken livers, onions and parsley. Sauté until livers are evenly browned and cooked through. Transfer to blender or food processor container. Add wine, TABASCO® Sauce and salt; cover. Process until smooth. Pour into decorative crock-style jar with lid. Chill until thick enough to spread. Serve with crackers or French bread.

Makes about 2 cups pâté

Smoked Salmon Roses

Crab Canapés

2/3 cup fat-free cream cheese, softened

2 teaspoons lemon juice

1 teaspoon hot pepper sauce

1 package (8 ounces) imitation crabmeat or lobster, flaked

1/3 cup chopped red bell pepper

2 green onions with tops, sliced (about 1/4 cup)

64 cucumber slices (about 2 1/2 medium cucumbers cut into 3/8-inch-thick slices) or melba toast rounds

Fresh parsley for garnish (optional)

1. Combine cream cheese, lemon juice and hot pepper sauce in medium bowl; mix well. Stir in crabmeat, bell pepper and green onions; cover. Chill until ready to serve.

2. When ready to serve, spoon 1 1/2 teaspoons crabmeat mixture onto each cucumber slice. Place on serving plate; garnish with parsley, if desired.   *Makes 16 servings*

54

Cook's Note

To allow flavors to blend, chill crab mixture at least 1 hour before spreading onto cucumbers or melba toast rounds.

Crab Canapés

Marinated Antipasto

1 cup julienne-cut carrots

1 cup fresh green beans, cut into 2-inch pieces

1 cup fresh Brussels sprouts, quartered

1 cup thinly sliced baby yellow squash

$\frac{1}{2}$ cup thinly sliced red bell pepper

$\frac{1}{2}$ cup thinly sliced yellow bell pepper

1 can (9 ounces) artichoke hearts, drained and quartered

2 cups water

$\frac{1}{2}$ cup white wine vinegar

1 tablespoon olive oil

1 teaspoon sugar

2 bay leaves

1 clove garlic

6 sprigs fresh thyme

$\frac{1}{4}$ teaspoon black pepper

$\frac{1}{2}$ cup chopped green onions with tops

$\frac{1}{2}$ cup minced fresh parsley

Peel of 2 oranges, cut into thin strips

1. Bring 4 cups water to a boil in large saucepan over high heat. Add carrots, beans and Brussels sprouts; cover and simmer 1 minute. Add squash and bell peppers; cover and simmer 1 minute or until vegetables are crisp-tender. Remove from heat; drain. Place vegetables and artichoke hearts in heatproof bowl.

2. Combine 2 cups water, vinegar, oil, sugar, bay leaves, garlic, thyme and black pepper in medium saucepan. Bring to a boil over medium heat. Pour over vegetables; mix well. Cool completely. Cover and refrigerate 12 hours or up to 3 days before serving.

3. Before serving, drain vegetables. Discard bay leaves, garlic and thyme. Toss vegetables with green onions, parsley and orange peel.   *Makes 8 servings*

Marinated Antipasto

Roasted Eggplant & Walnut Tomato Caps

1 eggplant (about 1 pound), cut into 1-inch chunks

1 green bell pepper, halved, seeded and sliced

1 onion, sliced

$1/4$ cup red or white wine vinegar

1 teaspoon dried basil *or* 2 tablespoons chopped fresh basil

$1/3$ cup chopped California walnuts

1 tablespoon capers

Salt and pepper to taste

24 large (golf-ball sized) cherry tomatoes (about 1 pound)

Preheat oven to 350°F. Coat a large baking pan with nonstick cooking spray. Spread eggplant, pepper and onion on prepared pan and bake until vegetables have wilted and browned lightly, stirring once, about 45 minutes. Cool to room temperature.

Place roasted vegetables in a food processor with the vinegar and basil; process until coarsely chopped. Add walnuts and capers and process until mixture is thick and coarsely blended. Season with salt and pepper.

Slice off the stem end of each tomato. Scoop out seeds and juices with a small spoon, leaving just the shell. Place a generous tablespoon of eggplant mixture in each tomato, mounding it over the top. Alternatively, place eggplant mixture in a plastic bag; seal, and cut off a corner of the bag. Pipe eggplant mixture into the tomatoes.

Makes 6 servings

Favorite recipe from **Walnut Marketing Board**

Smoked Salmon, Olive and Herb Tartine

1 (8-ounce) French bread baguette
4 ounces nonfat cream cheese, softened
1 1/2 tablespoons lemon juice
1/2 cup sliced California Ripe Olives
3 tablespoons minced fresh chives
2 tablespoons minced fresh tarragon
2 cups mixed baby lettuce
8 ounces sliced smoked salmon
2 shallots, minced
1 tablespoon lemon zest

1. Slice baguette in half lengthwise and toast in 400°F oven for 5 minutes until golden. Cut each half into 4 pieces.

2. Using the paddle attachment, beat cream cheese and lemon juice in the bowl of an electric mixer for 3 to 4 minutes, stopping and scraping down side of bowl often. Mix until fluffy.

3. Fold 1/4 cup California Ripe Olives, chives and tarragon into cream cheese mixture.

4. Assemble tartines by spreading 1/3 cup olive-cream cheese onto each baguette piece. Top with 1/4 cup lettuce and 1 ounce smoked salmon. Garnish the tops with shallots, remaining 1/4 cup California Ripe Olives and lemon zest. Serve 2 slices per person.   *Makes 4 servings*

Favorite recipe from **California Olive Industry**

Mini Tuna Tarts

- 1 (3-ounce) pouch of **STARKIST** Flavor Fresh Pouch® Albacore or Chunk Light Tuna
- 2 tablespoons mayonnaise
- 2 tablespoons sweet pickle relish
- 1 green onion, including top, minced
- ¾ cup shredded Monterey Jack cheese
- Salt and pepper to taste
- 1 package (10 count) refrigerated flaky biscuits

Combine tuna, mayonnaise, pickle relish, onion and cheese; mix well. Add salt and pepper. Separate each biscuit into 2 halves. Press each half in bottom of lightly greased muffin pan to form a cup. Spoon scant tablespoon tuna mixture into each muffin cup. Bake in preheated 400°F oven 8 to 10 minutes or until edges of biscuits are just golden. Serve hot or cold.

Makes 20 servings

Prep Time: 15 minutes

Mini Tuna Tarts

Tiny Vegetable Boats

1 can (15 ½ ounces) reduced-sodium chick-peas (garbanzo beans), rinsed and drained

¼ cup fresh lemon juice

2 ounces reduced-sodium fat-free chicken broth

1 large clove garlic, peeled

¼ teaspoon white pepper

¼ teaspoon dried thyme leaves

16 white mushrooms

¼ cup thinly sliced roasted sweet red pepper

16 medium-size grape or cherry tomatoes

16 fresh snow pea pods

1. Process chickpeas, lemon juice, broth, garlic, white pepper and thyme in food processor fitted with chopping blade until mixture is smooth, stopping to scrape down side of work bowl. Transfer mixture to small bowl; cover and refrigerate.

2. Wash, dry and stem mushrooms. Scoop out caps slightly with small melon ball scoop or tip of vegetable peeler. (Reserve stems and trimmings in plastic bag for later use.) Using teaspoon, fill each mushroom cap with chickpea mixture, mounding slightly. Place mushrooms on 10-inch serving plate. Score filling with tines of fork and garnish each with 1 strip of red pepper cut to fit. Cover loosely with plastic wrap; refrigerate until ready to serve.

3. Halve tomatoes lengthwise. Using tip of vegetable peeler, scrape out seeds, juice and membranes. Place tomato halves face down on paper towels to dry. Using teaspoon, fill tomato halves with chickpea mixture, mounding slightly. Place on serving plate. Cover loosely with plastic wrap; refrigerate until ready to serve.

4. Wash, dry and trim snow pea pods. Spread remaining chickpea mixture on curved side of each pod. Place on serving plate. If desired, score filling lengthwise with tines of fork. Cover loosely with plastic wrap; refrigerate until ready to serve.

Makes 48 appetizers or 16 servings

Tiny Vegetable Boats

Smoked Salmon Lavash

4 ounces cream cheese, softened
1 tablespoon lemon juice
1/4 teaspoon prepared horseradish
4 small (about 5 inches) lavash
4 ounces sliced smoked salmon
1/2 red onion, thinly sliced
2 tablespoons capers, drained

Combine cream cheese, lemon juice and horseradish in small bowl. Spread carefully over lavash. Top with salmon, onion and capers. *Makes 4 servings*

Brie Torte

1 (15- to 16-ounce) wheel Brie cheese
6 tablespoons butter, softened
1/3 cup chopped dried tart cherries
1/4 cup finely chopped pecans
1/2 teaspoon dried thyme *or* 2 teaspoons finely chopped fresh thyme

Refrigerate Brie until chilled and firm or freeze 30 minutes until firm. Cut Brie in half horizontally.

Combine butter, cherries, pecans and thyme in small bowl; mix well. Spread mixture evenly onto cut side of one half of Brie. Top with other half, cut side down. Lightly press together. Wrap in plastic wrap; refrigerate 1 to 2 hours. To serve, cut into serving size wedges and bring to room temperature. Serve with water crackers.

Makes about 20 appetizer servings

Note: If wrapped securely in plastic wrap, this appetizer will keep in the refrigerator for at least one week.

Favorite recipe from **Cherry Marketing Institute**

Smoked Salmon Lavash

Roasted Garlic Hummus

2 tablespoons Roasted Garlic (recipe follows)
1 can (15 ounces) chick-peas (garbanzo beans), rinsed and drained
1/4 cup fresh parsley, stems removed
2 tablespoons lemon juice
2 tablespoons water
1/2 teaspoon curry powder
3 drops dark sesame oil
   Dash hot pepper sauce
   Pita bread and fresh vegetables (optional)

Prepare Roasted Garlic. Place chick-peas, parsley, Roasted Garlic, lemon juice, water, curry powder, sesame oil and hot pepper sauce in food processor or blender; process until smooth, scraping down side of bowl once. Serve with pita bread triangles and fresh vegetables, if desired.

Makes 6 (1/4-cup) servings

Roasted Garlic: Cut off top third of 1 large head garlic (not the root end) to expose cloves; discard top. Place head of garlic, trimmed end up, on 10-inch square of foil. Rub garlic generously with olive oil and sprinkle with salt. Gather foil ends together and close tightly. Roast in preheated 350°F oven 45 minutes or until cloves are golden and soft. When cool enough to handle, squeeze roasted garlic cloves from skins; discard skins.

Roasted Garlic Hummus

Lipton® Roasted Red Pepper & Onion Dip

1 envelope LIPTON® RECIPE SECRETS® Onion Soup Mix*
1 container (16 ounces) regular or light sour cream
1 jar (7 ounces) roasted red peppers, drained and chopped

*Also terrific with LIPTON® RECIPE SECRETS® Savory Herb with Garlic Soup Mix.

1. In small bowl, combine all ingredients; chill at least 2 hours.

2. Serve with your favorite dippers.   *Makes 2 cups dip*

Vegetable Cream Cheese

1 envelope LIPTON® RECIPE SECRETS® Vegetable Soup Mix
2 packages (8 ounces each) cream cheese, softened
2 tablespoons milk

1. In medium bowl, combine all ingredients; chill 2 hours.

2. Serve on bagels or with assorted fresh vegetables.   *Makes 2 1/2 cups spread*

Prep Time: 10 minutes ✦ Chill Time: 2 hours

69

Lipton® Roasted Red Pepper & Onion Dip

Cucumber-Dill Dip

Salt

1 cucumber, peeled, seeded and finely chopped

6 green onions, white parts only, chopped

1 cup plain yogurt

1 package (3 ounces) reduced-fat cream cheese

2 tablespoons fresh dill *or* 1 tablespoon dried dill weed

Fresh dill sprigs

1. Lightly salt cucumber in small bowl; toss. Refrigerate 1 hour. Drain cucumber; dry on paper towels. Return cucumber to bowl and add onions. Set aside.

2. Place yogurt, cream cheese and dill in food processor or blender; process until smooth. Stir into cucumber mixture. Cover; refrigerate 1 hour. Spoon dip into individual plastic cups with lids or serving bowl; garnish with fresh dill sprigs, if desired.

Makes about 2 cups dip

70

Hot Artichoke Dip

1 cup mayonnaise

1 cup sour cream

$\frac{1}{4}$ cup grated Parmesan cheese

$\frac{1}{4}$ cup chopped roasted red peppers

1 can (14 ounces) artichoke hearts, drained and chopped

1 $\frac{1}{3}$ cups *French's*® French Fried Onions, divided

Assorted crackers or bagel chips

1. Preheat oven to 375°F. Combine mayonnaise, sour cream, cheese, roasted peppers, artichokes and $\frac{2}{3}$ *cup* French Fried Onions. Spoon into 9-inch pie plate.

2. Bake 25 minutes or until hot. Top with remaining $\frac{2}{3}$ *cup* onions and bake 5 minutes or until onions are golden. Serve with assorted crackers or bagel chips.

Makes 3 cups dip

Cucumber-Dill Dip

Hearty Calico Bean Dip

¾ **pound ground beef**

½ **pound sliced bacon, crisp-cooked and crumbled**

1 **can (16 ounces) baked beans**

1 **can (15 ounces) Great Northern beans, rinsed and drained**

1 **can (15 ounces) kidney beans, rinsed and drained**

1 **small onion, chopped**

½ **cup brown sugar**

½ **cup ketchup**

1 **tablespoon vinegar**

1 **teaspoon prepared yellow mustard**

Tortilla chips

Slow Cooker Directions

1. Brown ground beef in large nonstick skillet, stirring to separate meat. Drain and discard fat. Spoon meat into slow cooker.

2. Add bacon, beans, onion, brown sugar, ketchup, vinegar and mustard to slow cooker; mix well.

3. Cover; cook on LOW 4 hours or on HIGH 2 hours. Serve with tortilla chips.

Makes 12 servings

Serving Suggestion: Place in serving dish and scoop up dip with tortilla chips.

Hearty Calico Bean Dip

Olive Tapenade Dip

1 ½ cups **(10-ounce jar)** pitted kalamata olives

3 tablespoons olive oil

3 tablespoons *French's*® **Bold n' Spicy Brown Mustard**

1 tablespoon minced fresh rosemary leaves *or* 1 teaspoon dried rosemary leaves

1 teaspoon minced garlic

1. Place all ingredients in food processor. Process until puréed.

2. Serve with vegetable crudités or pita chips.   *Makes 4 (¼-cup) servings*

Prep Time: 10 minutes

Cook's Note

To pit olives, place in plastic bag. Gently tap with wooden mallet or rolling pin until olives split open. Remove pits.

Olive Tapenade Dip

Zesty Pesto Cheese Spread and Dip

2 packages (8 ounces each) cream cheese, softened

1 cup shredded mozzarella cheese

1 cup chopped fresh basil or parsley

$1/2$ cup grated Parmesan cheese

$1/2$ cup pine nuts, toasted

$1/3$ cup *French's*® *Gourmayo*™ Sun Dried Tomato Light Mayonnaise

1 teaspoon minced garlic

1. Combine all ingredients in food processor. Cover and process until smooth and well blended.

2. Spoon pesto spread into serving bowl or crock. Spread on crackers or serve with vegetable crudités.   *Makes 12 ($1/4$-cup) servings*

Tip: To toast pine nuts, place nuts on baking sheet. Bake at 350°F for 8 to 10 minutes or until lightly golden or microwave on HIGH (100%) 1 minute.

Prep Time: 15 minutes

Zesty Pesto Cheese Spread and Dip

Hidden Valley® Bacon-Cheddar Ranch Dip

1 container (16 ounces) sour cream (2 cups)
1 packet (1 ounce) HIDDEN VALLEY® The Original Ranch® Dips Mix
1 cup (4 ounces) shredded Cheddar cheese
¼ cup crisp-cooked, crumbled bacon*
   Potato chips or corn chips, for dipping

Bacon pieces can be used.

Combine sour cream and dips mix. Stir in cheese and bacon. Garnish as desired. Chill at least 1 hour. Serve with chips.   *Makes about 3 cups dip*

Tangy Cheese Dip

1 container (8 ounces) whipped cream cheese
¼ cup milk
3 tablespoons *French's®* Bold n' Spicy Brown Mustard or *French's®* Sweet & Tangy Honey Mustard
2 tablespoons mayonnaise
2 tablespoons minced green onions

1. Combine all ingredients; mix until well blended.

2. Serve with vegetables or chips.   *Makes 5 (¼-cup) servings*

Prep Time: 15 minutes

78

Hidden Valley® Bacon-Cheddar
Ranch Dip

Spinach Dip

1 package (10 ounces) frozen chopped spinach, thawed and squeezed dry
1 container (16 ounces) sour cream
1 cup HELLMANN'S® or BEST FOODS® Mayonnaise
1 package KNORR® Recipe Classics™ Vegetable Soup, Dip and Recipe Mix
1 can (8 ounces) water chestnuts, drained and chopped (optional)
3 green onions, chopped

✦ In medium bowl, combine all ingredients; chill at least 2 hours to blend flavors.

✦ Stir before serving. Serve with your favorite dippers.

Makes about 4 cups dip

Yogurt Spinach Dip: Substitute 1 container (16 ounces) plain lowfat yogurt for sour cream.

Spinach and Cheese Dip: Add 2 cups (8 ounces) shredded Swiss cheese with spinach.

Prep Time: 10 minutes ✦ *Chill Time*: 2 hours

Ortega® 7-Layer Dip

1 can (16 ounces) ORTEGA® Refried Beans
1 package (1.25 ounces) ORTEGA Taco Seasoning Mix
1 container (8 ounces) sour cream
1 container (8 ounces) refrigerated guacamole
1 cup (4 ounces) shredded cheddar cheese
1 cup ORTEGA Salsa-Homestyle Recipe (Mild)
1 can (4 ounces) ORTEGA Diced Green Chiles
2 large green onions, sliced
   Tortilla chips

COMBINE beans and seasoning mix in small bowl. Spread bean mixture in 8-inch square baking dish.

TOP with sour cream, guacamole, cheese, salsa, chiles and green onions. Serve with chips.

Makes 10 to 12 servings

Cook's Note

This dip can be prepared up to 2 hours ahead and refrigerated.

Texas Pecan and Beef Dip

Nonstick cooking spray

$^1/_2$ **cup pecan pieces**

3 **tablespoons thinly sliced green onions with tops**

1 **package (8 ounces) cream cheese, softened and cut into cubes**

3 **ounces lager beer**

$^1/_2$ **jar (2.2 ounces) dried beef, rinsed in hot water, drained and cut into** $^1/_4$**-inch pieces**

1 $^1/_2$ **teaspoons BBQ seasoning blend**

Breadsticks, pita bread and assorted fresh vegetables for dipping

1. Spray bottom of small saucepan generously with cooking spray; heat over medium heat until hot. Add pecans and onions; cook over medium heat 3 to 5 minutes or until pecans are toasted and onions are tender.

2. Add cream cheese and lager to saucepan; cook over medium-low heat until cheese is melted. Stir in dried beef and BBQ seasoning; cook over medium-high heat, stirring constantly, until hot.

3. Spoon dip into bowl; sprinkle with additional green onion tops, if desired. Serve with dippers. *Makes 8 (3-tablespoon) servings*

Prep and Cook Time: 18 minutes

Texas Pecan and Beef Dip

Lipton® Onion Dip

1 envelope LIPTON® RECIPE SECRETS® Onion Soup Mix
1 container (16 ounces) sour cream

1. In medium bowl, combine ingredients; chill, if desired.
2. Serve with your favorite dippers.   *Makes 2 cups dip*

Salsa Onion Dip: Stir in ½ cup of your favorite salsa.

Prep Time: 5 minutes

Lipton® Ranch Dip

1 envelope LIPTON® RECIPE SECRETS® Ranch Soup Mix
1 container (16 ounces) sour cream

1. In medium bowl, combine ingredients; chill, if desired.
2. Serve with your favorite dippers.   *Makes 2 cups dip*

Ranch Salsa Dip: Stir in ½ cup of your favorite salsa.

Ranch Artichoke Dip: Stir in 1 jar (14 ounces) marinated artichoke hearts, drained and chopped.

Prep Time: 5 minutes

Top to bottom: Lipton® Onion Dip and
Lipton® Ranch Dip

Creamy Dill Veggie Dip

4 ounces reduced-fat cream cheese

2 tablespoons fat-free (skim) milk

$1/2$ package dry ranch salad dressing mix (about 2 tablespoons)

1 $1/2$ teaspoons dried dill weed *or* 1 tablespoon fresh dill

4 cups raw vegetables (such as cherry tomatoes, celery sticks, baby carrots, broccoli florets, cucumber slices, zucchini slices and/or red or green bell pepper strips)

8 unsalted breadsticks

1. Place cream cheese, milk, dressing mix and dill weed in blender; blend until smooth. Store, tightly sealed, in refrigerator.

2. Serve dip with vegetables and breadsticks. *Makes 8 servings*

Note: This recipe can be doubled, if needed.

Cook's Note

For a quick portable snack, divide dip among 8 individual plastic containers; cover tightly. Divide vegetables and breadsticks among 8 small resealable plastic bags. Store in cooler with ice.

Creamy Dill Veggie Dip

Party Cheese Spread

- 1 cup ricotta cheese
- 6 ounces cream cheese, softened
- 1 medium onion, chopped
- 2 tablespoons grated Parmesan cheese
- 1 tablespoon drained capers
- 2 anchovy fillets, mashed *or* 2 teaspoons anchovy paste
- 1 teaspoon dry mustard
- 1 teaspoon paprika
- 1/2 teaspoon hot pepper sauce
- Red cabbage or bell pepper for serving container

1. Beat ricotta cheese and cream cheese in large bowl with electric mixer at medium speed until well blended. Stir in onion, Parmesan cheese, capers, anchovies, mustard, paprika and hot pepper sauce; mix well. Cover; refrigerate at least 1 day or up to 1 week to allow flavors to blend.

2. Just before serving, remove and discard any damaged outer leaves from cabbage. Slice small piece from bottom so cabbage will sit flat. Cut out and remove inside portion of cabbage, leaving a 1-inch-thick shell. (Be careful not to cut through bottom of cabbage.) Spoon dip into hollowed-out cabbage. Garnish, if desired.

Makes about 2 cups spread

Party Cheese Spread

Decorative Rice Mold

2 tablespoons butter or margarine

1/2 cup chopped onion

4 cups chicken broth

2 cups uncooked long-grain white rice

1 tablespoon dried parsley flakes

2 teaspoons dried basil leaves

1 teaspoon dried oregano leaves

1/2 teaspoon salt

1/2 teaspoon ground turmeric

1/2 teaspoon black pepper

5 or 6 green onion tops, blanched*

1 large carrot, peeled, diagonally sliced and blanched*

1 large radish, thinly sliced

1/2 cup (2 ounces) grated Parmesan cheese

*To blanch green onion tops and carrots, fill medium saucepan with water. Bring to a boil. Add carrots; cook 2 minutes. Add green onions; cook 1 to 2 minutes longer. Drain. Immediately transfer to bowl of ice water to stop cooking process. Set aside.

1. Melt butter in large saucepan. Add onion; cook and stir until tender. Stir in broth, rice, parsley, basil, oregano, salt, turmeric and pepper. Bring to a boil. Reduce heat to medium-low. Cover; simmer 20 to 25 minutes or until rice is tender.

2. Meanwhile, spray 6-cup soufflé dish or round casserole dish with nonstick cooking spray. Using sharp knife or scissors, cut green onion tops into leaf and stem shapes; cut carrot and radish slices into flower shapes. Set aside.

3. When rice is cooked, remove saucepan from heat; stir in cheese. Spoon into prepared dish; press down firmly to compact rice mixture. Let stand 10 minutes.

4. Invert dish onto serving platter; gently shake to loosen rice, if necessary. Remove dish. Decorate with green onion tops and carrot and radish slices as shown in photo. Garnish, if desired. Serve warm. *Makes 10 to 12 servings*

Decorative Rice Mold

Nutty Carrot Spread

¼ **cup finely chopped pecans**

6 **ounces fat-free cream cheese, softened**

2 **tablespoons frozen orange juice concentrate, thawed**

¼ **teaspoon ground cinnamon**

1 **cup shredded carrot**

¼ **cup raisins**

36 **party pumpernickel bread slices, toasted, or melba toast rounds**

1. Preheat oven to 350°F. Place pecans on ungreased baking sheet. Bake 10 minutes or until lightly toasted, stirring occasionally.

2. Meanwhile, combine cream cheese, orange juice concentrate and cinnamon in small bowl; stir until well blended. Stir in carrot, pecans and raisins.

3. Spread about 1 tablespoon cream cheese mixture onto each bread slice. Garnish, if desired.   *Makes 18 servings*

Cook's Note

To soften cream cheese quickly, remove from wrapper and place in medium microwave-safe bowl. Microwave at Medium (50% power) 15 to 20 seconds or until slightly softened.

Nutty Carrot Spread

Festive Cranberry Mold

½ cup water
1 package (6 ounces) raspberry-flavored gelatin
1 can (8 ounces) cranberry sauce
1 ⅔ cups cranberry juice cocktail
1 cup sliced bananas (optional)
½ cup walnuts, toasted (optional)

Bring water to a boil in medium saucepan over medium-high heat. Add gelatin and stir until dissolved. Fold in cranberry sauce. Reduce heat to medium; cook until sauce is melted. Stir in cranberry juice cocktail.

Refrigerate mixture until slightly thickened. Fold in banana slices and walnuts, if desired. Pour mixture into 4-cup mold; cover and refrigerate until gelatin is set.

Makes 8 servings

Pecan Cheese Ball

2 packages (8 ounces each) cream cheese, softened
1 package shredded Cheddar cheese (about 8 ounces)
1 envelope LIPTON® RECIPE SECRETS® Onion Soup Mix
2 tablespoons finely chopped fresh parsley
½ teaspoon garlic powder
½ cup finely chopped pecans, toasted if desired

1. In large bowl, with electric mixer, beat cream cheese until light and fluffy, about 2 minutes. Stir in Cheddar cheese, soup mix, parsley and garlic powder.

2. Wet hands with cold water. Roll cheese mixture into ball. Roll cheese ball in pecans until evenly coated.

3. Refrigerate 1 hour or until set. Serve with crackers.

Makes 1 cheese ball

Prep Time: 15 minutes ◆ Chill Time: 1 hour

Festive Cranberry Mold

Robust Cheddar, Feta and Walnut Cheese Ball

8 ounces (2 cups) grated California Cheddar cheese

8 ounces (1 cup) cream cheese

4 ounces (¾ cup) crumbled California feta cheese

2 cloves garlic, minced

¼ teaspoon salt

¼ teaspoon hot pepper sauce

1 cup chopped California walnuts, toasted if desired, divided

2 tablespoons capers, drained

2 tablespoons chopped, roasted and peeled red bell pepper

2 tablespoons gin or vodka (optional)

Pinch cayenne pepper

Combine Cheddar cheese, cream cheese, feta cheese, garlic, salt and pepper sauce; mix until blended and smooth. Add ½ cup walnuts, capers, bell pepper and gin, if desired. Continue to mix until ingredients are incorporated and evenly blended. Mixture will be easier to shape if refrigerated 2 to 3 hours before forming.

Add cayenne pepper to remaining ½ cup walnuts and toss to coat. Spread nuts on sheet of waxed paper.

With damp hands, divide cheese mixture in half. Pat and press each half into ball about 3 inches across or into log about 5 inches long and 2 inches wide. (Shape does not need to be perfect.)

If desired, roll each ball or log in walnuts, patting coating in firmly. Wrap in plastic wrap and chill until ready to serve. *Makes 12 servings*

Feta and Fontina Walnut Cheese Ball: Omit the Cheddar and cream cheeses and substitute 8 ounces (2 cups) grated California Fontina cheese and 4 ounces (1 cup) grated California Mozzarella cheese. Combine with the feta cheese and other ingredients as directed above. If desired, roll the balls or logs in a mixture of ¼ cup chopped parsley and ¼ cup dry bread crumbs or rye cracker crumbs.

Favorite recipe from **Walnut Marketing Board**

Alouette® Elégante® with Red Pepper Coulis

1 small jar roasted red peppers, drained
1 teaspoon olive oil
1 (6-ounce) package **ALOUETTE®** Elégante®, Roasted Garlic and Pesto
  Paprika
  Chopped fresh chives or parsley

To make red pepper coulis, add roasted red peppers and olive oil to food processor; purée until smooth. Pour coulis into center of 8-inch rimmed salad plate (a plain white plate works best). Position Alouette Elégante in center of coulis. Sprinkle paprika and chopped chives around rim of plate. Serve with your favorite crusty bread.

Makes 6 to 8 servings

Cook's Note

This spread is also great served with fresh cut vegetables such as carrots, cucumbers and celery.

Molded Crab Mousse

2 cans (6 ounces each) crabmeat *or* 2 cups fresh shelled crabmeat

1 cup (4 ounces) shredded Colby cheese

1/2 cup finely chopped celery

1/4 cup finely chopped onion

1/4 cup finely chopped red bell pepper

1/4 cup finely chopped green bell pepper

1 cup sour cream

1/2 cup mayonnaise

1/4 cup chili sauce

2 tablespoons fresh lemon juice

3 tablespoons cold water

1 tablespoon unflavored gelatin

Cucumber slices (optional)

Fresh dill sprigs (optional)

1. Lightly oil 1-quart fish-shaped or other shaped mold.

2. Place crabmeat in large bowl. Toss with cheese, celery, onion and bell peppers.

3. Combine sour cream, mayonnaise, chili sauce and lemon juice in small bowl. Pour cold water into small saucepan; stir in gelatin. Cook over low heat, stirring constantly, until thoroughly dissolved. Stir quickly into sour cream mixture.

4. Fold sour cream mixture into crab mixture; spoon into prepared mold. Cover with plastic wrap; refrigerate 3 hours or until set. Unmold onto serving platter. Garnish with cucumber slices and dill sprigs, if desired.

Makes 32 appetizer servings (2 tablespoons each)

Molded Crab Mousse

Bacon Cheese Spread

1/2 cup **FLEISCHMANN'S®** Original Margarine, softened

1/4 cup grated Parmesan cheese

1/4 cup real bacon bits

1/4 cup minced onion

1. Blend margarine, cheese, bacon and onion in small bowl with mixer at medium speed. Cover and store in refrigerator.

2. Serve as a topping for baked potatoes or as a spread for toasted Italian bread.

Makes about 1 cup spread

Preparation Time: 10 minutes ✦ Total Time: 10 minutes

Pineapple Lime Mold

1 can (20 ounces) **DOLE®** Pineapple Chunks

2 packages (3 ounces each) lime gelatin

2 cups boiling water

1 cup sour cream

1/2 cup chopped walnuts

1/2 cup chopped **DOLE®** Celery

Drain pineapple chunks, reserving syrup. Dissolve gelatin in boiling water. Add sour cream and reserved syrup. Chill until slightly thickened. Stir in pineapple chunks, walnuts and celery. Pour into 7-cup mold. Chill until set.

Makes 8 servings

Bacon Cheese Spread

Cheddar Cheese and Rice Roll

2 cups cooked UNCLE BEN'S® ORIGINAL CONVERTED® Brand Rice

3 cups grated low-fat Cheddar cheese

¾ cup fat-free cream cheese, softened

1 can (4½ ounces) green chilies, drained, chopped

⅛ teaspoon hot sauce

1½ cups chopped walnuts

PREP: CLEAN: Wash hands. Combine rice, Cheddar cheese, cream cheese, chilies and hot sauce. Mix by hand or in food processor. Shape mixture into a log. Roll in walnuts. Wrap tightly with plastic wrap and refrigerate 1 hour.

SERVE: Serve with assorted crackers.

CHILL: Refrigerate leftovers immediately.   *Makes 15 servings*

Prep Time: 20 minutes ✦ Cook Time: none

Cheddar Cheese and Rice Roll

Hot Artichoke and Tuna Spread

- 1 (3-ounce) pouch of STARKIST Flavor Fresh Pouch® Albacore or Chunk Light Tuna
- 1 jar (12 ounces) marinated artichoke hearts, drained
- 1 cup shredded mozzarella cheese
- 1/2 cup grated Parmesan cheese
- 1/4 cup chopped canned green chilies
- 1 to 2 cloves garlic
- 2 to 3 tablespoons mayonnaise
- 1 tablespoon minced green onion
-   Hot pepper sauce to taste
-   French bread or assorted crackers

In food processor bowl with metal blade, place all ingredients except bread. Process until well blended but not puréed. Transfer mixture to ovenproof serving dish. Bake, uncovered, in preheated 350°F oven about 30 minutes or until mixture is golden. Serve hot with French bread.

Makes 12 servings

Note: This mixture may be baked in small hollowed bread shell. Wrap in foil; bake as above. Open top of foil last 5 minutes of baking.

Tip: Mixture keeps well, tightly covered, in refrigerator for up to 5 days.

Prep Time: 35 minutes

Mandarin Orange Mold

1 ¾ cups boiling water

2 packages (4-serving size each) orange flavor gelatin

3 cups ice cubes

1 can (15 ¼ ounces) DOLE® Tropical Fruit Salad, drained

1 can (11 ounces) DOLE® Mandarin Oranges, drained

✦ Stir boiling water into gelatin in large bowl at least 2 minutes until completely dissolved. Add ice cubes. Stir until ice is melted and gelatin is thickened. Stir in fruit salad and mandarin oranges. Spoon into 6-cup mold.

✦ Refrigerate 4 hours or until firm. Unmold. (See Cook's Note.) Garnish as desired.

Makes 12 servings

Prep Time: 15 minutes ✦ Chill Time: 4 hours

Cook's Note

To unmold, dip mold in warm water about 15 seconds. Gently pull gelatin from around edges with moist fingers. Place moistened serving plate on top of mold. Invert mold and plate. Holding mold and plate together, shake slightly to loosen. Gently remove mold.

Roasted Red Pepper Spread

I cup roasted red peppers, rinsed and drained
I package (8 ounces) cream cheese, softened
I packet (I ounce) HIDDEN VALLEY® The Original Ranch® Salad Dressing
   & Seasoning Mix
Baguette slices and sliced ripe olives (optional)

Blot dry red peppers. In a food processor fitted with a metal blade, combine peppers, cream cheese and salad dressing & seasoning mix; process until smooth. Spread on baguette slices and garnish with olives, if desired.   *Makes 2 cups spread*

Crabmeat Spread

I package (8 ounces) light cream cheese, softened
¼ cup cocktail sauce
I package (8 ounces) imitation crabmeat
Cocktail rye bread or assorted crackers

Spread cream cheese evenly on serving plate. Pour cocktail sauce over cream cheese; top with imitation crabmeat.

Serve with cocktail rye bread.   *Makes 1½ cups spread (12 servings)*

Prep Time: 5 minutes

107

Roasted Red Pepper Spread

Seafood Spread

1 package (8 ounces) cream cheese, softened
½ pound smoked whitefish, skinned, boned and flaked
2 tablespoons minced green onion
1 tablespoon plus 1 teaspoon chopped fresh dill
1 teaspoon lemon juice
¼ teaspoon black pepper
   Rye bread slices (optional)
   Lime wedges for garnish (optional)

1. Beat cream cheese in medium bowl with electric mixer at medium speed until smooth. Add whitefish, green onion, dill, lemon juice and black pepper; mix until well blended. Refrigerate until ready to serve.

2. Serve with rye bread slices and garnish with lime wedges, if desired.

Makes 12 servings (1½ cups)

Prep Time: 10 minutes plus refrigeration

Cook's Note

To flake the whitefish, use a fork to break off small pieces or layers of the fish.

Seafood Spread

Herbed Blue Cheese Spread with Garlic Toasts

1 ⅓ cups low-fat (1%) cottage cheese

1 ¼ cups (5 ounces) crumbled blue, feta or goat cheese

1 large clove garlic

2 teaspoons lemon juice

2 green onions with tops, sliced (about ¼ cup)

¼ cup chopped fresh basil or oregano *or* 1 teaspoon dried basil or oregano leaves

2 tablespoons toasted slivered almonds*

Garlic Toasts (recipe follows)

To toast almonds, spread in single layer on baking sheet. Bake in preheated 350°F oven 8 to 10 minutes or until golden brown, stirring frequently.

1. Combine cottage cheese, blue cheese, garlic and lemon juice in food processor. Cover; process until smooth. Add green onions, basil and almonds; pulse until well blended but still chunky.

2. Spoon cheese spread into small serving bowl; cover. Refrigerate until ready to serve.

3. When ready to serve, prepare Garlic Toasts. Spread 1 tablespoon cheese spread onto each toast slice. Garnish, if desired.   *Makes 16 servings*

Garlic Toasts

32 (½-inch-thick) slices French bread

Nonstick cooking spray

¼ teaspoon garlic powder

⅛ teaspoon salt

Place bread slices on nonstick baking sheet. Lightly coat both sides of bread slices with cooking spray. Combine garlic powder and salt in small bowl; sprinkle evenly onto bread slices. Broil 6 to 8 inches from heat 30 to 45 seconds on each side or until bread slices are lightly toasted on both sides.   *Makes 32 pieces*

Herbed Blue Cheese Spread with Garlic Toasts

Shrimp Paté

¹/₂ pound cooked peeled shrimp

¹/₄ cup (¹/₂ stick) unsalted butter, cut into chunks

2 teaspoons dry vermouth or chicken broth

1 teaspoon lemon juice

1 teaspoon Dijon mustard

¹/₄ teaspoon salt

¹/₄ teaspoon ground mace

¹/₈ teaspoon ground red pepper

¹/₈ teaspoon freshly ground black pepper

¹/₂ cup chopped pistachio nuts

2 large heads Belgian endive

1. Combine shrimp, butter, vermouth, lemon juice, mustard, salt, mace, ground red pepper and black pepper in blender or food processor. Blend to a purée. Remove. If mixture is too soft to handle refrigerate 1 hour.

2. Spread pistachio nuts on sheet of waxed paper. Gently form mixture into 8-inch log. Roll in nuts to coat. Chill 1 to 3 hours. Separate endive into individual leaves and serve with shrimp log.   *Makes 12 (2-tablespoon) servings*

Variation: Spoon shrimp paté into serving bowl and sprinkle with pistachio nuts.

Shrimp Paté

Best of the Wurst Spread

    1 tablespoon butter or margarine
1/2 cup finely chopped onion
    1 package (16 ounces) liverwurst
1/4 cup mayonnaise or salad dressing
1/4 cup finely chopped dill pickle
    2 teaspoons prepared horseradish or spicy brown mustard
    1 tablespoon drained capers
    2 teaspoons dried dill weed
1/4 small dill pickle, cut into strips (optional)
    Crackers or cocktail rye bread

1. Heat butter in small saucepan over medium heat until melted. Add onion; cook and stir 5 minutes or until tender. Mash liverwurst with fork in medium bowl; beat in onion, mayonnaise, chopped dill pickle, prepared horseradish, capers and dill weed.

2. Form liverwurst mixture into football shape on serving plate; decorate with dill pickle strips to look like football laces, if desired. Serve with crackers.

Makes 12 (3-tablespoon) servings

Serve It With Style!: For added flavor, serve this spread with mustard toast instead of rye bread. To prepare mustard toast, lightly spread prepared horseradish or spicy brown mustard on cocktail rye bread slices. Broil, 4 inches from heat, until lightly browned.

Prep and Cook Time: 15 minutes

THE
GOAL
IS
FUN!

Best of the Wurst Spread

Roasted Eggplant Spread

1 large eggplant

1 can (14 1/2 ounces) diced tomatoes, drained

1/2 cup finely chopped green onions

1/2 cup chopped fresh parsley

2 tablespoons red wine vinegar

1 tablespoon olive oil

3 cloves garlic, finely chopped

1/2 teaspoon salt

1/2 teaspoon dried oregano leaves

2 (8-inch) pita bread rounds

Fresh lemon and lime slices for garnish (optional)

1. Preheat oven to 375°F.

2. Place eggplant on baking sheet. Bake 1 hour or until tender, turning occasionally. Remove eggplant from oven. Let stand 10 minutes or until cool enough to handle.

3. Cut eggplant in half lengthwise; remove pulp. Place pulp in medium bowl; mash with fork until smooth. Add tomatoes, onions, parsley, vinegar, oil, garlic, salt and oregano; blend well. Cover eggplant mixture; refrigerate 2 hours.

4. Preheat broiler. Split pita bread rounds horizontally in half to form 4 rounds. Stack rounds; cut into sixths to form 24 wedges. Place wedges on baking sheet. Broil, 4 inches from heat, 3 minutes or until crisp.

5. Serve eggplant spread with warm pita bread wedges. Garnish with lemon and lime slices, if desired.

Makes 4 servings

Roasted Eggplant Spread

Zesty Pesto Cheese Spread

2 packages (8 ounces each) cream cheese, softened

1 cup shredded mozzarella cheese

1 cup chopped fresh basil or parsley

$1/2$ cup grated Parmesan cheese

$1/2$ cup toasted pine nuts*

$1/3$ cup *French's*® Honey Dijon Mustard

1 clove garlic

*To toast pine nuts, place nuts on baking sheet. Bake at 350°F 8 to 10 minutes or until lightly golden or microwave on microwavable dish on HIGH (100%) 1 minute.

1. Combine cream cheese, mozzarella, basil, Parmesan, pine nuts, mustard and garlic in food processor. Cover and process until smooth and well blended.

2. Spoon pesto spread into serving bowl or crock. Spread on crackers or serve with vegetable crudités.   *Makes 3$1/4$ cups spread*

Serving Variations: Pesto spread may also be piped into cherry tomatoes using pastry bag fitted with decorative tip. Or, use as filling in rolled flour tortillas.

Prep Time: 15 minutes

Cheddar Cheese Spread

3 ounces white Cheddar cheese, diced

3 ounces yellow Cheddar cheese, diced

1 package (3 ounces) cream cheese, cubed

6 green onions, white parts only, finely chopped

2 tablespoons butter or margarine, softened

2 tablespoons dry sherry

1 teaspoon Worcestershire sauce

1 teaspoon Dijon mustard

1/4 teaspoon salt (optional)

Dash hot pepper sauce (optional)

2 tablespoons finely chopped fresh chives

Assorted crackers

Place all ingredients except chives and crackers in food processor or blender; process until smooth. Add chives; pulse to mix. Cover; refrigerate. Allow spread to soften at room temperature before serving. Serve with crackers.

Makes about 2 cups spread

Cook's Note

To give Cheddar Cheese Spread as a gift, place cheese mixture in a crock or gift container before refrigerating. Include a box of crackers.

Pesto-Cheese Logs

¹/₃ **cup walnuts, toasted***

1 **package (8 ounces) cream cheese, softened**

¹/₃ **cup prepared pesto**

¹/₃ **cup crumbled feta cheese**

2 **teaspoons cracked black pepper**

2 **tablespoons finely shredded carrot**

2 **tablespoons chopped fresh parsley**

Assorted crackers

Carrot slivers, parsley and fresh thyme for garnish (optional)

To toast walnuts, spread in single layer on baking sheet. Bake in preheated 350°F oven 8 to 10 minutes or until golden brown, stirring frequently.

Process walnuts in food processor using on/off pulsing action until walnuts are ground, but not pasty. Remove from food processor; set aside.

Process cream cheese, pesto and feta cheese in food processor until smooth. Spread ³/₄ cup cheese mixture on waxed paper and form 4-inch log. Wrap waxed paper around cheese log. Repeat with remaining cheese mixture. Refrigerate logs at least 4 hours or until well chilled. Roll each chilled log to form 5-inch log.

Combine walnuts and pepper. Roll 1 log in nut mixture to coat. Combine carrot and parsley. Roll remaining log in carrot mixture to coat. Serve immediately or wrap and refrigerate up to 1 day before serving. To serve, thinly slice log and serve with crackers. Garnish, if desired. *Makes 2 logs*

Pesto-Cheese Logs

Celebration Cheese Ball

2 packages (8 ounces) cream cheese, softened

$1/3$ cup mayonnaise

$1/4$ cup grated Parmesan cheese

2 tablespoons finely chopped carrot

1 tablespoon finely chopped red onion

1 $1/2$ teaspoons prepared horseradish

$1/4$ teaspoon salt

$1/2$ cup chopped pecans or walnuts

Assorted crackers and breadsticks

Combine all ingredients except pecans and crackers in medium bowl. Cover and refrigerate until firm.

Shape cheese mixture into ball; roll in pecans. Wrap cheese ball in plastic wrap and refrigerate at least 1 hour. Serve with assorted crackers and breadsticks.

Makes about 2$1/2$ cups spread

Celebration Cheese Ball

Chutney Cheese Spread

2 packages (8 ounces each) fat-free cream cheese, softened

1 cup (4 ounces) shredded reduced-fat Cheddar cheese

1/2 cup mango chutney

1/4 cup thinly sliced green onions with tops

3 tablespoons dark raisins, chopped

2 cloves garlic, minced

1 to 1 1/2 teaspoons curry powder

3/4 teaspoon ground coriander

1/2 to 3/4 teaspoon ground ginger

1 tablespoon chopped dry roasted peanuts

Additional green onions and melba toast (optional)

1. Place cream cheese and Cheddar cheese in food processor or blender; process until smooth. Stir in chutney, sliced green onions, raisins, garlic, curry powder, coriander and ginger. Cover; refrigerate 2 to 3 hours.

2. Just before serving, sprinkle peanuts over spread. Serve spread with additional green onions and melba toast, if desired. *Makes 20 (2-tablespoon) servings*

Cook's Tip: The spread can also be garnished with 1 tablespoon toasted coconut to provide a slightly sweeter flavor.

Chutney Cheese Spread

Hot Pepper Cranberry Jelly Appetizer

1/2 cup canned whole cranberry sauce

1/4 cup apricot fruit spread

1 teaspoon sugar

1 teaspoon cider vinegar

1/2 teaspoon red pepper flakes

1/2 teaspoon grated fresh ginger

Crackers and cheeses

1. Combine cranberry sauce, fruit spread, sugar, vinegar and red pepper flakes in small saucepan. Cook over medium heat until sugar is dissolved. (Do not boil.) Transfer to bowl to cool completely. Stir in ginger.

2. To serve, top crackers with cheese and a dollop of cranberry-apricot mixture.

Makes 16 appetizer servings

Roasted Eggplant Spread with Focaccia

1 eggplant (1 pound)

1 medium tomato

1 tablespoon fresh lemon juice

1 tablespoon chopped fresh basil *or* 1 teaspoon dried basil leaves

2 teaspoons chopped fresh thyme *or* 3/4 teaspoon dried thyme leaves

1 clove garlic, minced

1/4 teaspoon salt

1 tablespoon extra virgin olive oil

Focaccia (recipe follows)

1. Preheat oven to 400°F. Poke holes in several places in eggplant with fork. Place on oven rack; bake 10 minutes. Meanwhile, cut stem end from tomato. Place tomato in small baking pan; place in oven with eggplant. Bake vegetables 40 minutes.

2. Cool vegetables slightly; peel. Cut eggplant into large slices. Place tomato and eggplant in food processor or blender. Add lemon juice, basil, thyme, garlic and salt; process until well blended. Slowly drizzle oil through feed tube and process until mixture is well blended. Refrigerate 3 hours or overnight.

3. To serve, spread 1 tablespoon spread on each focaccia wedge. Garnish with cherry tomato wedges and additional fresh basil, if desired. *Makes 10 servings*

Focaccia

¾ cup warm water (110° to 115°F)

1 ½ teaspoons sugar

1 teaspoon active dry yeast

1 tablespoon extra-virgin olive oil

1 teaspoon salt

1 teaspoon dried rosemary

1 cup all-purpose flour

1 cup whole wheat flour

Nonstick cooking spray

1. Pour water into large bowl. Dissolve sugar and yeast in water; let stand 10 minutes or until bubbly. Stir in oil, salt and rosemary. Add flours, ½ cup at a time, stirring until dough begins to pull away from side of bowl and forms ball.

2. Turn dough onto lightly floured surface and knead 5 minutes or until dough is smooth and elastic, adding more all-purpose flour if necessary. Place dough in bowl lightly sprayed with cooking spray and turn dough so all sides are coated. Cover with towel or plastic wrap and let rise in warm, draft-free place about 1 hour or until doubled in bulk.

3. Turn dough onto lightly floured surface and knead 1 minute. Divide into 3 balls; roll each into 6-inch circle. Using fingertips, dimple surfaces of dough. Place on baking sheet sprayed with cooking spray; cover and let rise 30 minutes.

4. Preheat oven to 400°F. Spray tops of dough circles with cooking spray; bake about 13 minutes or until golden brown. Remove from oven and cut each loaf into 10 wedges. *Makes 10 servings (30 wedges)*

Hip Party Snacks

Sweet and Spicy Snack Mix

> **6** cups popped popcorn
>
> **3** cups miniature pretzels
>
> **1 ½** cups pecan halves
>
> **⅔** cup packed brown sugar
>
> **⅓** cup butter or margarine
>
> **1** teaspoon ground cinnamon
>
> **¼** teaspoon ground red pepper

Microwave Directions

1. Combine popped corn, pretzels and nuts in large bowl.

2. Place brown sugar, butter, cinnamon and red pepper in 2-cup microwavable cup. Microwave at HIGH 1 ½ minutes or until bubbly.

3. Pour butter mixture over popcorn mixture; toss with rubber spatula until well mixed.

Makes about 1 0 cups snack mix

Prep and Cook Time: 1 2 minutes

Sweet and Spicy Snack Mix

Parmesan-Pepper Crisps

2 cups (4 ounces) loosely packed coarsely-grated Parmesan cheese
2 teaspoons freshly ground black pepper

1. Preheat oven to 400°F. Line wire racks with paper towels.

2. Place heaping teaspoonfuls cheese 2 inches apart on ungreased nonstick baking sheet. Flatten cheese mounds slightly with back of spoon. Sprinkle each mound with pinch of pepper.

3. Bake 15 to 20 minutes or until crisps are very lightly browned. (Watch closely—crisps burn easily.) Let cool on baking sheet 2 minutes; carefully remove with spatula to prepared racks. Store in airtight container in refrigerator up to 3 days.

Makes about 26 crisps

Cook's Note

To curl crisps like a potato chip, remove from baking sheet immediately and drape over rolling pin. Let cool for 1 minute; remove to prepared racks.

Parmesan-Pepper Crisps

Rosemary-Scented Nut Mix

2 tablespoons unsalted butter

2 cups pecan halves

1 cup unsalted macadamia nuts

1 cup walnuts

1 teaspoon dried rosemary

$\frac{1}{2}$ teaspoon salt

$\frac{1}{4}$ teaspoon red pepper flakes

1. Preheat oven to 300°F. Melt butter in large saucepan over low heat. Add pecans, macadamia nuts and walnuts; mix well. Add rosemary, salt and red pepper flakes; cook and stir about 1 minute.

2. Pour mixture onto ungreased nonstick baking sheet. Bake 15 minutes, stirring mixture occasionally. Let cool completely. *Makes 32 servings*

Rosemary-Scented Nut Mix

Crispy Bacon Sticks

$1/2$ cup (1 $1/2$ ounces) grated Wisconsin Parmesan cheese, divided

5 slices bacon, halved lengthwise

10 breadsticks

Microwave Directions

Spread $1/4$ cup cheese on plate. Press one side of bacon slice into cheese; wrap diagonally around breadstick with cheese-coated side toward stick. Place on paper plate or microwave-safe baking sheet lined with paper towels. Repeat with remaining bacon slices, cheese and breadsticks. Microwave on HIGH 4 to 6 minutes until bacon is cooked, checking for doneness after 4 minutes. Roll again in remaining $1/4$ cup Parmesan cheese. Serve warm.   *Makes 10 sticks*

Favorite recipe from **Wisconsin Milk Marketing Board**

Nutty Onion Snack Mix

　 1 can (**6 ounces**) *French's*® French Fried Onions
　 2 cups mixed nuts
1 ¹/₂ cups small pretzel twists
　 2 cans (1 ¹/₂ ounces each) *French's*® Potato Sticks
　 3 tablespoons butter or margarine, melted
　 3 tablespoons *French's*® Bold n' Spicy Brown Mustard

1. Place French Fried Onions, nuts, pretzels and potato sticks in 4-quart microwave-safe bowl. Combine butter and mustard. Pour over mixture in bowl; toss well to coat evenly.

2. Microwave, uncovered, on HIGH for 6 minutes, stirring well every 2 minutes. Transfer to paper towels; cool completely.　　　　*Makes about 9 cups snack mix*

Prep Time: 5 minutes ✦ Cook Time: 6 minutes

Nicole's Cheddar Crisps

1 ³/₄ cups all-purpose flour

¹/₂ cup yellow cornmeal

³/₄ teaspoon sugar

³/₄ teaspoon salt

¹/₂ teaspoon baking soda

¹/₂ cup (1 stick) butter or margarine

1 ¹/₂ cups (6 ounces) shredded sharp Cheddar cheese

¹/₂ cup cold water

2 tablespoons white vinegar

Coarsely ground black pepper

1. Combine flour, cornmeal, sugar, salt and baking soda in large bowl. Cut in butter with pastry blender or two knives until mixture resembles coarse crumbs. Stir in cheese, water and vinegar with fork until mixture forms soft dough. Cover dough; refrigerate 1 hour or until firm.*

2. Preheat oven to 375°F. Grease 2 large baking sheets. Divide dough into 4 pieces. Roll each piece into paper-thin circle (about 13 inches in diameter) on floured surface. Sprinkle with pepper; press pepper firmly into dough.

3. Cut each circle into 8 wedges; place on prepared baking sheets. Bake about 10 minutes or until crisp. Store in airtight container for up to 3 days.

Makes 32 crisps

Dough may be frozen at this point for later use. To prepare, thaw in refrigerator and proceed as directed.

Nicole's Cheddar Crisps

Original Ranch® Snack Mix

8 cups **KELLOGG'S® CRISPIX®*** cereal

2 ½ cups **small pretzels**

2 ½ cups **bite-size Cheddar cheese crackers (optional)**

3 tablespoons **vegetable oil**

1 packet (1 ounce) **HIDDEN VALLEY® The Original Ranch® Salad Dressing & Seasoning Mix**

*Kellogg's® and Crispix® are registered trademarks of Kellogg Company.

Combine cereal, pretzels and crackers in a gallon-size Glad® Zipper Storage Bag. Pour oil over mixture. Seal bag and toss to coat. Add salad dressing & seasoning mix; seal bag and toss again until coated. *Makes 10 cups snack mix*

Original Ranch® Oyster Crackers

1 box (16 ounces) **oyster crackers**

¼ cup **vegetable oil**

1 packet (1 ounce) **HIDDEN VALLEY® The Original Ranch® Salad Dressing & Seasoning Mix**

Place crackers in a gallon-size Glad® Fresh Protection Bag. Pour oil over crackers. Seal bag and toss to coat. Add salad dressing & seasoning mix; seal bag and toss again until coated. Spread evenly on large baking sheet. Bake at 250°F for 15 to 20 minutes. *Makes 8 cups crackers*

Top to bottom: Original Ranch® Snack Mix and Original Ranch® Oyster Crackers

Honey-Roasted Bridge Mix

1/2 **cup honey**

2 **tablespoons butter or margarine**

1 **teaspoon ground cinnamon, divided**

4 **cups mixed nuts**

2 to 3 **tablespoons superfine sugar**

Preheat oven to 325°F. Combine honey, butter and 1/2 teaspoon cinnamon in saucepan. Bring mixture to a boil; cook 2 minutes, stirring constantly. Pour honey mixture over nuts; stir well until nuts are coated. Spread nut mixture onto foil-lined cookie sheet or jelly-roll pan.

Bake 10 to 15 minutes or until nuts are glazed and lightly browned. Do not allow nuts to burn. Cool 20 to 30 minutes; remove from foil. Combine sugar and remaining 1/2 teaspoon cinnamon; toss with glazed nuts to coat.   *Makes 4 cups mix*

Prep Time: About 15 minutes ✦ Bake Time: About 15 minutes

Favorite recipe from **National Honey Board**

Roasted Nuts from Hidden Valley®

1 pound assorted unsalted nuts, such as pecans, walnuts or mixed nuts

1/4 cup maple syrup

2 tablespoons light brown sugar

1 packet (1 ounce) HIDDEN VALLEY® The Original Ranch® Salad Dressing & Seasoning Mix

Place nuts in plastic bag; add maple syrup and coat well. Sprinkle sugar and salad dressing & seasoning mix over nuts. Coat well. Spread nuts in single layer on greased baking pan. Bake at 250°F for 35 minutes. Transfer immediately to large bowl. Cool, stirring to separate.

Makes about 4 cups nuts

Seasoned Snack Mix

1 cup natural whole almonds

1 tablespoon instant minced onion

2 to 3 tablespoons butter or margarine

Grated peel of 1 SUNKIST® lemon

1 tablespoon dried parsley leaves

1/2 teaspoon seasoned salt

1/2 teaspoon garlic salt

4 cups assorted bite-size cereals

Small Cheddar cheese crackers or pretzel sticks

In large skillet, sauté almonds and onion in butter until lightly toasted. Add lemon peel, parsley, seasoned salt and garlic salt; mix well. Add cereals and crackers; heat, stirring until well coated with butter mixture. Cool.

Makes about 5 cups snack mix

Herb Cheese Twists

2 tablespoons butter or margarine
¼ cup grated Parmesan cheese
1 teaspoon dried parsley flakes
1 teaspoon dried basil leaves
1 can (7½ ounces) refrigerated buttermilk biscuits

1. Preheat oven to 400°F. Lightly grease baking sheet.

2. Microwave butter in small microwavable bowl at MEDIUM (50% power) just until melted; cool slightly. Stir in cheese, parsley and basil. Set aside.

3. Pat each biscuit into 5×2-inch rectangle. Spread 1 teaspoon butter mixture onto each rectangle; cut in half lengthwise. Twist each strip 3 or 4 times. Place on prepared baking sheet. Bake 8 to 10 minutes or until golden brown.   *Makes 5 servings*

Cut the time: Save even more time by using ready-to-bake breadsticks. Spread the butter mixture onto the breadsticks, then bake them according to the package directions.

Prep and Cook Time: 20 minutes

Herb Cheese Twists

Party Mix

3 cups bite-size rice cereal

2 cups O-shaped oat cereal

2 cups bite-size shredded wheat cereal

1 cup peanuts or pistachios

1 cup thin pretzel sticks

$^1/_2$ cup (1 stick) butter, melted

1 tablespoon Worcestershire sauce

1 teaspoon seasoned salt

$^1/_2$ teaspoon garlic powder

$^1/_8$ teaspoon ground red pepper (optional)

Slow Cooker Directions

1. Combine cereals, nuts and pretzels in slow cooker.

2. Mix melted butter, Worcestershire sauce, seasoned salt, garlic powder and red pepper, if desired, in small bowl. Pour over cereal mixture in slow cooker; toss lightly to coat.

3. Cover; cook on LOW 3 hours, stirring well every 30 minutes. Remove cover; cook an additional 30 minutes. Store in airtight container.   *Makes 10 cups snack mix*

Party Mix

Southwest-Spiced Walnuts

2 cups California walnuts

1 tablespoon sugar

1 teaspoon sea salt

$\frac{1}{2}$ teaspoon garlic powder

$\frac{1}{2}$ teaspoon ground cumin

$\frac{1}{4}$ teaspoon cayenne pepper

1 tablespoon walnut oil

Preheat oven to 375°F. Plunge walnuts into a pot of boiling water, turn off heat and let stand 2 minutes; drain. Spread walnuts on baking sheet and roast 10 minutes. Measure seasonings in a small bowl and stir to combine. Heat oil in a skillet. Add walnuts and toss 1 minute. Add seasoning mixture and toss until walnuts are well coated. Cool on a paper towel.   *Makes 2 cups nuts*

Favorite recipe from **Walnut Marketing Board**

146

Cook's Note

Store unshelled nuts in a cool, dry and dark place. Heat, light and moisture encourage rancidity. Stored properly, they can be kept for several months. Shelled nuts will keep in an airtight container up to 4 months refrigerated and 6 months if frozen.

Deviled Mixed Nuts

3 tablespoons vegetable oil

2 cups assorted unsalted nuts, such as peanuts, almonds, Brazil nuts or walnuts

2 tablespoons sugar

1 teaspoon paprika

$^1/_2$ teaspoon chili powder

$^1/_2$ teaspoon curry powder

$^1/_2$ teaspoon ground cumin

$^1/_2$ teaspoon ground coriander

$^1/_2$ teaspoon black pepper

$^1/_4$ teaspoon salt

Heat oil in large skillet over medium heat; cook and stir nuts in hot oil 2 to 3 minutes or until browned. Combine remaining ingredients in small bowl; sprinkle over nuts. Stir to coat evenly. Heat 1 to 2 minutes more. Drain nuts on wire rack lined with paper towels. Serve warm.

Makes 2 cups nuts

Southwest Snack Mix

- **4 cups corn cereal squares**
- **2 cups unsalted pretzels**
- **$\frac{1}{2}$ cup unsalted pumpkin or squash seeds**
- **1 $\frac{1}{2}$ teaspoons chili powder**
- **1 teaspoon minced fresh cilantro or parsley**
- **$\frac{1}{2}$ teaspoon garlic powder**
- **$\frac{1}{2}$ teaspoon onion powder**
- **1 egg white**
- **2 tablespoons olive oil**
- **2 tablespoons lime juice**

1. Preheat oven to 300°F. Spray large nonstick baking sheet with nonstick cooking spray.

2. Combine cereal, pretzels and pumpkin seeds in large bowl. Combine chili powder, cilantro, garlic powder and onion powder in small bowl.

3. Whisk together egg white, oil and lime juice in separate small bowl. Pour over cereal mixture; toss to coat evenly. Add seasoning mixture; mix lightly to coat evenly. Transfer to prepared baking sheet.

4. Bake 45 minutes, stirring every 15 minutes; cool. Store in airtight container.

Makes about 12 ($\frac{1}{2}$-cup) servings

Variation: Substitute $\frac{1}{2}$ cup unsalted peanuts for pumpkin seeds.

148

Southwest Snack Mix

Peppy Snack Mix

3 (3-inch) plain rice cakes, broken into bite-size pieces
1 ½ cups bite-size frosted shredded wheat biscuit cereal
¾ cup pretzel sticks, halved
3 tablespoons reduced-fat margarine, melted
2 teaspoons reduced-sodium Worcestershire sauce
¾ teaspoon chili powder
⅛ to ¼ teaspoon ground red pepper

Preheat oven to 300°F. Combine rice cake pieces, cereal and pretzels in 13×9-inch baking pan. Combine margarine, Worcestershire, chili powder and red pepper in small bowl. Drizzle over cereal mixture; toss to combine. Bake 20 minutes, stirring after 10 minutes.   *Makes 6 (⅔-cup) servings*

150

Spiced Nuts

1 egg white
2 tablespoons sugar
1 teaspoon ground cinnamon
½ teaspoon ground allspice
1 ¾ cups pecan halves

1. Preheat oven to 325°F. Grease baking sheet; set aside.

2. Beat egg white in small bowl with electric mixer at high speed until soft peaks form. Beat in sugar, cinnamon and allspice. Stir in pecans until coated.

3. Spread pecans on prepared baking sheet, separating pecans. Bake about 12 minutes or until crisp. Let stand until cool.   *Makes about ¼ pound nuts*

Peppy Snack Mix

Easy Italian No-Bake Snack Mix

3 tablespoons olive oil

1 tablespoon dried Italian seasoning

4 cups small bow tie pretzels

1 can (12 ounces) cocktail peanuts

1 box (7 ounces) baked crispy snack crackers

1/4 cup grated Parmesan cheese

1. Combine oil and seasoning in large resealable plastic food storage bag; knead well.

2. Add pretzels, peanuts and crackers. Seal bag; shake gently to coat well with oil mixture. Add cheese. Seal bag; shake gently to coat. Snack mix can be stored in bag up to 5 days.   *Makes 10 cups snack mix*

Prep Time: 10 minutes

Sesame Tortilla Crackers

2 tablespoons olive oil

1 tablespoon sesame seeds

1/4 teaspoon onion powder

6 flour tortillas (6 inches in diameter)

Preheat oven to 450°F. Combine olive oil, sesame seeds and onion powder in small bowl. Brush oil mixture on one side of each tortilla, stacking tortillas oiled side up.

Cut tortilla stack into 6 wedges using sharp knife. Arrange wedges, oiled side up, in single layer on ungreased baking sheets.

Bake 6 to 8 minutes until crackers are golden brown. Transfer crackers to wire racks; cool completely. Store crackers in airtight container up to 3 days.

Makes 36 crackers

153

Easy Italian No-Bake Snack Mix

Acknowledgments

The publisher would like to thank the companies and organizations listed below for the use of their recipes and photographs in this publication.

Allen Canning Company

Alouette® Cheese, Chavrie® Cheese, Saladena®

California Olive Industry

Cherry Marketing Institute

Crisco is a registered trademark of The J.M. Smucker Company

Dole Food Company, Inc.

Fleischmann's® Margarines and Spreads

The Hidden Valley® Food Products Company

MASTERFOODS USA

McIlhenny Company (TABASCO® brand Pepper Sauce)

National Honey Board

National Pork Board

Ortega®, A Division of B&G Foods, Inc.

Reckitt Benckiser Inc.

Smucker's® trademark of The J.M. Smucker Company

Sonoma® Dried Tomatoes

StarKist Seafood Company

Reprinted with permission of Sunkist Growers, Inc.

Unilever Foods North America

Walnut Marketing Board

Wisconsin Milk Marketing Board

Index

Metric Conversion Chart

VOLUME MEASUREMENTS (dry)

$^1/_8$ teaspoon = 0.5 mL
$^1/_4$ teaspoon = 1 mL
$^1/_2$ teaspoon = 2 mL
$^3/_4$ teaspoon = 4 mL
1 teaspoon = 5 mL
1 tablespoon = 15 mL
2 tablespoons = 30 mL
$^1/_4$ cup = 60 mL
$^1/_3$ cup = 75 mL
$^1/_2$ cup = 125 mL
$^2/_3$ cup = 150 mL
$^3/_4$ cup = 175 mL
1 cup = 250 mL
2 cups = 1 pint = 500 mL
3 cups = 750 mL
4 cups = 1 quart = 1 L

VOLUME MEASUREMENTS (fluid)

1 fluid ounce (2 tablespoons) = 30 mL
4 fluid ounces ($^1/_2$ cup) = 125 mL
8 fluid ounces (1 cup) = 250 mL
12 fluid ounces (1$^1/_2$ cups) = 375 mL
16 fluid ounces (2 cups) = 500 mL

WEIGHTS (mass)

$^1/_2$ ounce = 15 g
1 ounce = 30 g
3 ounces = 90 g
4 ounces = 120 g
8 ounces = 225 g
10 ounces = 285 g
12 ounces = 360 g
16 ounces = 1 pound = 450 g

DIMENSIONS

$^1/_{16}$ inch = 2 mm
$^1/_8$ inch = 3 mm
$^1/_4$ inch = 6 mm
$^1/_2$ inch = 1.5 cm
$^3/_4$ inch = 2 cm
1 inch = 2.5 cm

OVEN TEMPERATURES

250°F = 120°C
275°F = 140°C
300°F = 150°C
325°F = 160°C
350°F = 180°C
375°F = 190°C
400°F = 200°C
425°F = 220°C
450°F = 230°C

BAKING PAN SIZES

Utensil	Size in Inches/Quarts	Metric Volume	Size in Centimeters
Baking or Cake Pan (square or rectangular)	8 × 8 × 2	2 L	20 × 20 × 5
	9 × 9 × 2	2.5 L	23 × 23 × 5
	12 × 8 × 2	3 L	30 × 20 × 5
	13 × 9 × 2	3.5 L	33 × 23 × 5
Loaf Pan	8 × 4 × 3	1.5 L	20 × 10 × 7
	9 × 5 × 3	2 L	23 × 13 × 7
Round Layer Cake Pan	8 × 1½	1.2 L	20 × 4
	9 × 1½	1.5 L	23 × 4
Pie Plate	8 × 1¼	750 mL	20 × 3
	9 × 1¼	1 L	23 × 3
Baking Dish or Casserole	1 quart	1 L	—
	1½ quart	1.5 L	—
	2 quart	2 L	—